Nancy Crown Preston

王光美

990.6.18
北京

Life Among the Minority
Nationalities of Northwest
Yunnan

CHINA'S NATIONALITIES SERIES

Life Among the Minority Nationalities of Northwest Yunnan

FOREIGN LANGUAGES PRESS   BEIJING

Photographer	Shen Che
Text	Shen Che and Lu Xiaoya
Editor	Liao Pin
Translator	Huang Weiwei
Art Editor	Chen Ting

First Edition　　1989

ISBN 0-8351-2222-0
ISBN 7-119-0056

Published by the Foreign Languages Press
24 Baiwanzhuang Road, Beijing, China

Distributed by China International Book Trading
Corporation (GUOJI SHUDIAN), P.O. Box 399, Beijing, China

Printed in the People's Republic of China

Contents

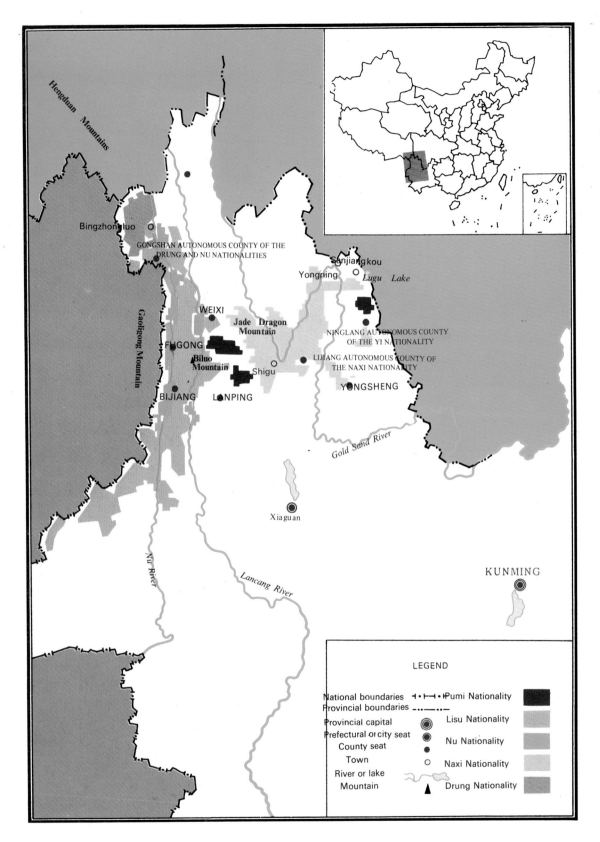

Bingzhongluo

GONGSHAN AUTONOMOUS COUNTY OF THE
DRUNG AND NU NATIONALITIES

Sanjiangkou

Yongning

Lugu Lake

WEIXI

Jade Dragon
Mountain

NINGLANG AUTONOMOUS COUNTY
OF THE YI NATIONALITY

FUGONG

Biluo
Mountain

Shigu

LIJIANG AUTONOMOUS COUNTY OF
THE NAXI NATIONALITY

BIJIANG

LANPING

YONGSHENG

Hengduan Mountains

Gaoligong Mountain

Gold Sand River

Xiaguan

Nu River

Lancang River

KUNMING

LEGEND

National boundaries ┼•┝━•┝ Pumi Nationality

Provincial boundaries ━•━•━

Provincial capital

Prefectural or city seat   Lisu Nationality

County seat

Town   Nu Nationality

River or lake

Mountain   ▲ Drung Nationality   Naxi Nationality

Shen Che, the photographer of this book, at Jasmine Pass on Gaoligong Mountain, the pass being 3,700 metres above sea level.

An Expedition into Northwest Yunnan

By Shen Che

When I left the bustle of exuberant Shanghai in 1980 to embark on a photographic tour on a bicycle, I myself had never thought I could become so strongly fascinated with Yunnan, a remote province of China. The dazzlingly colourful scenery along the southwestern border of our country, the earnest, liberal and unsophisticated nature and the radiant and beautiful national cultures common to our fraternal nationalities there, all combine to attract me like a magnet.

Within four years I went down to Yunnan three times, shuttling in the midst of the tropical jungles, gullies and ravines for an extensive coverage of these nationalities. I believe it is quite beyond my power to adequately recount the impressions connected with my visits there.

A strolling in moonlight on the bank of the Lancang River would not only bring serenity to my mind but also uplift me above all common run. While bathing in the early morning glow by the Lugu Lake, I felt as if I had shaken off my old mental slough and recast my physique.

Each time I chanced to be with a caravan herded by the men of one of these compatriot nationalities in a mountain several thousand metres above sea level and we cooked together around a bonfire, there arose a communion among us of the feelings of intimacy, warmth and concord. The burial and matrimonial rites, festivities consecrated with either fire or water, folk-songs joyous and sorrowful, customs old and new — all of which, I have witnessed in the multinational areas — have creatively left on me an indelible impression that is all hardly to efface, and have kindled a zeal in me for creating something artistic. Sentimentally I have already regarded Yunnan as my second native place.

In 1984, I sallied forth on a coverage journey into the Lijiang River valley area, the Gongshan Drung-Nu and Nu nationalities, Autonomous County, and the Nujiang Lisu Autonomous Prefecture in northwest Yunnan to gather first-hand information about the life of the Naxi, Pumi, Lisu, Drung, and Nu nationalities; and there I stayed for six months. Deep ravines and endlessly undulating snow-capped mountains make up the isolation of this region from the outside world and, therefore, transportation in these parts is extremely difficult. The Drung River Valley has all along posed an especial threat to wayfarers. These circumstances, however, were nothing more than a challenge to me. And I took it up with the conviction that to go for the Golden Fleece Jason has to embark on a dangerous voyage. In this mood I set out on my journey with the camera strapped on my back. . . .

The Yak Hill — Home of the Pumi People

The Jinsha River (the Gold Sand River) bisects the Hengduan Mountain Range (the Longitudinal Mountains) midway and rushes violently southward through the Qinghai-Tibet Highland until it comes to Shigu (a township in Lijiang County, Yunnan), where its current swings sharply towards the northeast. And it is right here that the river shapes itself into a wonderful bend. Since the Gold Sand River forms part of the upper reaches of the Yangtze River, it is popularly known as "the First Bend of the Yangtze." But not far away from here this capricious current of the Gold Sand River takes its second sharp turn at Sanjiangkou (in Ninglang Yi Autonomous County, Yunnan) where it begins to rush southward in such an unusual rapidity. And it is right here that the Gold Sand River wriggles itself into "the Second Bend of the Yangtze." In the east of the now south-running Gold Sand River and parallel to it, towers the Yak Hill, with a summit of more than 4,400 metres above sea level. The hill is one of the main communities populated by the Pumi nationality.

The densely-forested Yak Hill, over 4,400 metres above sea level, is situated in Ninglang County, Yunnan.

One of the many natural pastures on the Yak Hill. Every year after the spring thaw and when lush verdure is everywhere over the pastureland, the local people walk their horses and yaks there to graze. The herdsmen pass their nights there in makeshift tents or sheds called "herdsmen's nests."

My Pumi Host

One day He Shuiming, a young Pumi writer, asked me to pay him a visit; he came to my place expressly to accompany me to his home. So we set out on horseback in an early morning, leaving the shore of the Lugu Lake for the giddy height of the Yak Hill. When we climbed over the Tuokuaya Canyon, 3,200 metres above sea level, it was already dusk. Beyond the canyon were the stockaded villages of the Yi people; and from there onward were trails leading downhill — trails sandwiched by more and more impenetrable woods. In the woods were limpid rivulets and transparent ponds; the colour of the water in them contrasted strikingly with the ocherous colour of the muddy water in the villages on the other side of the canyon. The forest here was extremely alluring after rain, and the panorama was all one of luxuriant green. Both of us on our horses were like two little boats threading between the surges of a green sea.

When we arrived in Lazi, the stockaded village where He Shuiming lived, dusk had waned into darkness. There were only five Pumi households in this village. My host treated me, a guest coming from afar, very warmheartedly; he followed the Pumi convention of hospitality. He conducted me through his "log chamber," a chamber built with logs, to reach his "above-the-ground parlour" — a structure about two feet above the ground and occupying nearly one fourth of the total floor space of his residential quarters. The parlour where he seated me was reserved only for receiving his honoured guests.

All the household now began to get busy for the reception they were going to give me. His sister-in-law busied herself serving me the food that had been prepared especially for the occasion. The first delicacy she offered me was "potted tea"; then she dished up *zanba* (made with roasted highland barley flour, a staple food of the local people). After that, a big bowl of *suolima* wine. The potted tea is prepared by first baking a lump of brick tea in a little earthen jar baked only for this purpose and then pouring water into the jar and finally putting it over the fireplace to boil. The tea thus prepared is particularly fragrant. The suolima wine is usually made by fermenting the barley together with two medical herbs — usually the rough gentian (*Gentiana scabra*),

Shen Che, the photographer, calls on a Pumi family. The warmhearted hostess serves him delicacies such as highland barley *zanba*, honey, wine, and fruits.

A "log chamber."

Plows, rakes, and other farm tools are hung up against the wall when they are not used.

The loom is installed in the space underneath the log chamber; such an arrangement that saves upstairs space and puts the bulky loom in a place better illuminated by sunlight.

The houses of the local inhabitants are usually surrounded by flowers in full blossom.

growing in the perennially snow-capped high mountains, and the lily flourishing on the banks of the Gold Sand River. This kind of brew is the indispensable drink of the Pumi people.

The dinner, or rather a feast, was ready before I had finished my cup of the "potted tea." The table was laden with a steaming stewed chicken, lush and tender mushrooms, and home-made salted pork. The curing process of the home-made salted pork, my host told me, is like this: After a pig is dressed, eviscerated, and boned, its disemboweled belly is filled with salt, seeds of the Chinese prickly ash, and other condiments; then its slit belly is stitched up, and the whole cured pig is stored in a shaded and cool place to dry up.

Local tradition dictates that family members other than the host are not allowed to eat their dinner before the guest has had his to the full. So I had only the host to accompany me throughout the dinner. His 99-year-old granny grinned, as she watched me taking the food with relish, and spoke earnestly and joyfully to me in Pumi tongue. Interpreting for her, my friend told me that his granny was just urging me to eat freely and as much as possible.

His family finally came to eat their dinner. While they were at the table, I took a glance at the "log chamber." At the centre of the residential quarters was erected a wooden post, cuboid in shape. The local folk call it the "sky prop," where, they believe, their house spirit abides. The family fireplace squarely faced the "sky prop." An iron tripod for cooking purposes was mounted over it. Between the tripod and the wooden wall of the log chamber was set a square slab of stone, which is called the *guozhuang* — actually used as an altar for making offerings to the ancestors of the family. The Pumi people will not eat anything until they have first placed it on the guozhuang or the tripod to signify that they invite their ancestors to taste it first. Before they have a drink, they sprinkle a few drops of wine on the guozhuang or tripod by way of oblation. It is a taboo with the Pumi people to stride over the tripod; nor is it permissible to put anything unclean on it. Any misbehaviour involving the sacred tripod and guozhuang will be interpreted as a serious disrespect for the ancestors. While taking a meal, the male members of the family are seated on the right side and the female members on the left side of the fireplace. The oldest family member or the member occupying the position of first seniority in the family hierarchy is seated close to the guozhuang; and all others range by following the order of age or seniority in the family.

The Feast for Mountain Deities

The next day happened to be the Holy Feast for Mountain Deities observed by the Pumi people. All the inhabitants in the neighbouring villages went up Yak Hill on that day. According to traditions and historical records the Pumi nationality belonged to two branches of China's ancient nomads — the Di tribe and the Qiang tribe. Originally they lived on the Qinghai-Tibet Highland and were divided into nomadic groups roaming the area on the borderlands of Qinghai, Gansu, and Sichuan provinces. Later on, they gradually moved away from the frigid highland, pushed forward along the Hengduan Mountain Range and migrated into the warm and fertile land of lush vegetation. Probably they had already settled in the region now called the Xichang District, Sichuan, before the 7th century and emerged there as one of the influential nationalities. After the 13th century they gradually migrated into the highland of northwest Yunnan. At that time they were wont to "live midway up the hill and roof their sheds with boards"; they "levelled the slopes for farming" and "raised a large number of cattle and horses." Their way of living was "to stay where there was pasture and leave when the grass there was gone" — in a word, nomadism. At that time livestock raising still outweighed their other means of livelihood. As

The area populated by the Pumi nationality is enclosed by mountains. Raising livestock constitutes a major part of their economy and horse husbandry is their main line of production.

the level of the social productive forces developed, agriculture gradually began to occupy a major position.

The population of the Pumi nationality now amounts to 24,169, the principal areas of their inhabitation are in Laojun Hill in Nanping County and Yak Hill in Ninglang County, both counties being in Yunnan Province. These two areas are crisscrossed with high mountains whose average altitude is no less than 2,000 metres above sea level. Ninety per cent of their arable land is found on the mountains. Since they have to till and graze the nearby mountains, they declare that, of all the spirits, the mountain deities are the most sacred; the local people would never, they believe, be blessed with bumper harvests nor would there be thriving herds without the guardianship of these mountain deities. They maintain that if the deities are offended, they would release a deluge or ferocious, predatory beasts against them and their stock. Every stockaded village of the Pumi people worships its particular mountain god. And there is a cardinal mountain god, generally known as "Suoguonaba." Activities to worship the mountain deities are observed on the fifth, fifteenth, and twenty-fifth of every lunar month by the Pumi folks. I fortunately arrived at Lazi just in time for witnessing their observance of the Feast of the Cardinal Mountain God Suoguonaba, which takes place only once a year.

All the villagers must take part in the observance of the Feast of Suoguonaba. Not even the aged or infants, who are unable to walk up the hill, are allowed to be excepted from the rites but they don't have to climb up the hill in person. Their relatives may be delegated to negotiate the summit in their stead. And to validify the delegation, the following rituals must be performed: Two chunks of *zanba*, roasted highland barley flour cake, are placed several times on the heads and shoulders of those represented by the relatives who are going up the hill also on his or her behalf, in the hope that all the evil spirits, maladies, and scourges that are probably going to befall them might be switched and cling to the two pieces of zanba. While administering the caked zanba, the delegated pilgrim has also

to mumble incantations or prayers. After going through this preliminary, these zanba chunks will be borne by these delegated pilgrims up the hill and offered at the altar of the mountain god. And it is believed that by conducting such solemnities the aged or infants may be exempted from all kinds of disasters. My friend's father performed such solemnities for both his wife and grandson; and the evils that were supposedly destined to befall them were now believed to have thus been carried away by these zanba chunks.

Two days' journey was needed for the pilgrims from Lazi to reach Suoguonaba Peak to pay homage to the Cardinal Mountain God Suoguonaba. At the end of the first day of the pilgrimage, we passed the night at Ridazi "nest," a location more than 3,500 metres above sea level. By "nest" in the Pumi tongue it means a temporary lodge for the herdsmen who graze their yaks at high altitudes. Every such lodge generally includes one or two log chambers or sheds. When I finally arrived at Ridazi nest, I was really exhausted. But the extremely magnificent and attractive landscape at this high altitude was simply captivating. Due east from the nest lies the Lugu Lake resplendent in all its green and azure and the grand Lion Hill is close nearby standing guard over it. To the southeast of Ridazi is Wangha Hill, a place replete with such medical herbs as Chinese caterpillar fungus (*Cordyceps sinensis*), fritillary (*Fritillaria thunbergii*), and *chuanxiong* (*Ligusticum wallichii*). To the west, imposingly looms the elegant, immaculate, and snowy massif, the Jade Dragon Hill. The Gold Sand River picks its way forward boisterously between Wangha Hill and Jade Dragon Hill. Everywhere to be seen in the thick forest are the dangling pendants of green known as "tree-beard" locally. When viewed against the setting sun, the beard looks just like a draping translucent greenish gauze. The Pumi girls snatch the beard from the boughs and take plenty of such stuff home to rub their cooking pots clean with. A very thick layer of fallen leaves covers the ground of the pine forest. So when you walk upon it, it imparts to your feet the feeling as of treading on a soft carpet. Around the nest, scores of livestock browse quite at their ease, the little bells beneath their

Observing the Feast of the Mountain Deities, all the Pumi families in the village load their altars with food, wine, salted pork, salt, and flowers as offerings.

The *guozhuang* in front of the home altar. Domestic offerings have to be laid on the guozhuang too.

necks keep tinkling happily. Here in numerous clusters of verdure scattered over the field were the alluring deep red strawberries, which the Pumi people call the "milk fruits." When I was strolling in the field, I gathered and ate a lot of them with relish, feeling myself quite relaxed. Thanks to the bounteous and charming Nature for relieving me of my fatigue in this sweet way.

The day after, the pilgrims continued to move forward. Ahead there were even more precipitous mountains. The old people and children were mounted on the horse backs, and the rest of them just went on foot. Every step I took at the altitude of 4,000 metres above sea level was a strain for me as I was born and bred in the warm and smooth plain south of the Yangtze River. But the lively Pumi folk took the pilgrimage very lightly; they talked and laughed freely as they worked all their way up the steep hill. When they surged into an open place of level ground alive with a riot of wild flowers, they dismounted and unloaded their horses, and their young people promptly swung themselves into the saddles to start a horse race. The aged people were as much aflame as the younger ones; they also actively took part in the contest. Now the thumping of the hoofs, the deafening roars of the cheering groups, and the ringing peals of laughter of the spectators were shattering the agelong reign of silence in the forest.

On their way to Suoguonaba Peak they presented their offerings at the altars of two minor mountain gods, then resumed their pilgrimage towards Tuokuaya Canyon. The terrain near the canyon was so steep and looked so dangerous and terrifying that it seemed as if the horses would tumble down the precipice into the abyss below at any moment. However, it was only when we had crossed the canyon and reached the place where the altar of the Cardinal Mountain God Suoguonaba was that I came to realize why the Pumi people would travel such a rugged distance in two strenuous days to come here: The main peak of the Yak Hill lies not far from the altar of Suoguonaba. The site of the altar is bounded on all sides by

A column of pilgrims on their way to pay homage to the Mountain Deiti

Following the sounding of the conches, the rites of the Feast of Suoguonaba begin.

huge pine forests and extensive patches of azalea. On our way up we had seen azalea groves in places about 3,000 metres above sea level. Though the flowers here had already withered now, still it was not hard for me to imagine what a superb spectacle the place had been when the wild flowers here were in full bloom — the crimson wild calamus flowers, the violet rough gentian blades, and a host of anonymous wild flowering plants combined, so to speak, to spread a splendidly multi-coloured, huge carpet over the undulating slope. A lake covering dozens of · square kilometres lies placidly in this forested plateau. It looks chaste and resigned like a virgin. And this beautiful haven is consecrated to the worship of the Cardinal Mountain God.

A huge pile of stones surrounds a giant tree which symbolizes the said deity. Now the pilgrims heaped on it all the pine branches they had gathered on their way here. In addition, they also laid down some zanba chunks, fruits, suolima wine and other offerings. Then they set about bedecking the nearby trees with coloured paper slips and florid cloth strips. In this way they ornamented their Cardinal Mountain God. Now they began to blow conches. Woo . . . woo . . . the conches boomed low and solemnly and resounded from the surrounding hills and valleys. Following the sound of the conches the rites of the Feast of Suoguonaba were launched. An aged man officiated the ceremony and began to chant the prayers, pleading for the blessings from Suoguonaba. After that, the pilgrims kindled the pine branches, and all of them circled clockwise around the giant tree slowly. As they moved around the tree, they threw unhusked rice, corns, broad beans, and *zanba* pieces at the tree from time to time. They also sprinkled milk and wine on it. At last they knelt down and kowtowed to the tree. Thus ended the rites of worshipping Suoguonaba. There was an interesting episode to note. Some Pumi folks would bring to the altar their old and tattered clothes. There they would stretch them on slender bamboo poles and suspended the stretched clothes from the boughs of the trees. Then they would ask some old Pumi people to offer some zanba pieces, drop some unhusked grains, and say prayers before the hanging clothes. This, they believe, would have the magic power of exempting the owners of the ragged clothes from all latent evil influences. With this ritual over, they would be transferred to the forests near the altar. (And it was said that Suoguonaba would take pleasure in eliminating the transferred misfortune from the forests at his discretion.)

Hunting is prohibited on the day devoted to the Feast of Suoguonaba, because all the wild animals are believed to be the "livestock" kept by Suoguonaba. The Pumi people brought here cured meat, fresh pork, bean curd and vegetables for cooking purposes and eating in the open near the altar. Ordinarily young people under 25 are not allowed to use any alcoholic drinks. On New Year festivals or holidays they may be granted one or two mouthfuls of wine in case the patriarchs' permission is obtained. But the Feast of Suoguonaba provides an exception to this taboo. On this day it is compulsory for everybody to drink wine. Even I, a guest hailing from afar, was not exempted from this practice. After guzzling two bowls of suolima wine, I was fairly intoxicated.

Having completed the rites of the Feast of Suoguonaba, I started my downward journey with the caravan. We passed some highland pastures, Yaks were seen turned loose to graze in these pastures by the Pumi herdsmen. I figure that herding livestock at such high altitudes must make them feel both cheerful on the one hand and helplessly lonely on the other.

The pilgrims set about bedecking the Abode of Suoguonaba with coloured paper slips.

Pilgrims throwing grains of corn about the giant tree, which stands for Suoguonaba, the Cardinal Mountain God.

The pilgrims kneel down and kowtow to the giant tree symbolizing the Cardinal Mountain God Suoguonaba, praying for his blessings.

Life in a Pumi Stockaded Village

In Chinese historical documents, various names have been recorded for the Pumi nationality, such as "the western aborigines" or "Baju." Different tribes of the Pumi nationality living in different areas have different tribal names. With the consensus arrived at in 1960 by the whole Pumi nationality in China, the word "Pumi" was adopted and used ever since as the popular name of this ethnic group. The Pumi language belongs to the Qiang language group of the Tibetan-Burmese branch of the Sino-Tibetan language family. Most of the Pumi tribes now use the Chinese language. My sojourn in the stockaded village of Lazi helped me, with the assistance of my host as my interpreter, to gain an in-depth understanding of quite a bit of the customs and the current life of the Pumi people.

Besides breakfast and dinner, the Pumi people habitually have their morning tea and *shaowu* (lunch) every day. The morning tea of a Pumi family usually consists of salty potted tea and zanba cakes, with the initial boiling of the potted tea dedicated as an offering to their ancestors. And the shaowu comprises mostly food made of barley flour.

The Pumi people are very hospitable. A visitor, whether he is intimately related to the host or not, won't be seen to "stay long with an empty stomach." It means that the host won't let him leave before he has tasted something the host offers him. Honey is a precious food preserved especially for entertaining visitors coming from distant lands, distinguished guests, or maids who pay the host a visit for the first time. As I was a visitor coming from a very faraway place, I was treated to honey in almost every house I dropped in. The honey, as a rule, was taken directly from the beehive, and is unprocessed raw honey. The host would serve me the honey in a wooden bowl, and I ate it with a spoon. When I had consumed only half of the content in the bowl, the host would fill my bowl with zanba and knead the mixture in my bowl into a kind of honeyed zanba cake, which tasted surfeitingly sweet.

The transition of the Pumi nationality from nomadism to settled agricultural life was completed long, long ago. They grow wheat, buckwheat, corn, potato, or the like and their farming is generally conducted on a fallow basis. Apart from agriculture, animal husbandry is also an important sector of their economy. Their livestock includes mainly cattle, horses, mules, and sheep. They are still fond of hunting. The shady forests on the Yak Hill are found abundant with such wild animals as river deer, muntjacs, boars and black bears. A kind of catapult locally called *diannu* is used by the Pumi hunters. This kind of hunting device is usually installed where wild animals frequent. Once one of them touches its triggering rope, it automatically discharges a missile at the victim. Of course, for such petty creatures as Baihan chicken, a running noose on a string stranded of hairs from a horse tail mixed with hempen cord is quite enough.

The Pumi people have an immeasurable stock of hunting stories to entertain you. Their hunters are very familiar with the habits and characteristics of various wild animals. For example, a muntjac will flee the instant it gets a little frightened, even before it realizes whether or not there is really cause for such a fright. An experienced Pumi hunter will not leave the place, after it has fled. Instead, he will just stay hidden with his loaded gun, because the curious little thing will soon come back to the place where it has got panic-stricken to ascertain what has scared it. The hunter fires at the moment the retracing muntjac reappears before him. Then and there, the success is, of course, assured. After the Pumi hunters have captured a large animal in the mountain, they kill and skin it right there and carry the flayed game on a pole back to their village. They believe that if thay take back the quarry alive and kill it at home, their own livestock may die soon.

The Pumi people observe the following festivals: the Grand Spring Festival, the Grand Mid-January Festival and the Harvest Festival. The Grand Spring Festival is something like

Buckwheat is also one of the staples in the Pumi area.

Corn is the principal cereal produced in the area inhabited by the Pumi people. When it ripens, a Pumi host is proud to treat his guests to roasted ears of tender corn.

the Spring Festival (Lunar New Year) chiefly observed by the Han nationality, China's main nationality. The exact date and observance of this festival varies from one Pumi nationality area to another. On this occasion, the courts, the gates, and the rooftops of all the Pumi houses are customarily decorated with pine shoots or branches as a symbol of prosperity. At the first crow of the village cocks early in the daybreak on the Lunar New Year's Day all the shotguns of the villagers will go off and all the conches will be blown to greet the advent of the New Year. At this signal all the youth of the village will rush at top speed to the riverside to fetch water carried in casks borne on their backs. The one who first reaches the riverside and gets the water into his or her cask will allegedly enjoy good luck throughout the new year. Such various events as archery, horse race, playing on the swing and hunting birds are also popular among the villagers.

A boy or girl who comes to the age of 13 goes through the solemn ceremony of "putting on trousers" (for boys) or of "putting on a skirt" (for girls), which is actually a ceremony to acknowledge the manhood or womanhood of a 13-year-old. On such an occasion, a big fire is made in the fireplace of the house concerned. If the 13-year-old in the house is a girl, she will install herself next to the "female post" erected on the right side and in front of the fireplace. She stands with one foot standing on a sack of rice and the other foot on a hunk of salted pork. These two things are symbolic of a bumper harvest and wealth. In her right hand she holds earrings, strung beads, bracelets and other ornaments while a piece of flaxen cloth and a skein of flaxen yarn are held. The thingst in her hands are emblematic of her claim to a woman's right and also her obligation to her family. Her mother comes forth to take off her long flaxen gown, then dresses her up in a blouse and a long finely-pleated skirt and fastens the skirt with a belt around her waist. If it is a boy who is to undergo the ceremony, he is ordered to hold in his right hand a dagger, which is a symbol of bravery. And in his left palm is placed a silver dollar, which signifies wealth. His maternal uncle-in-law will come forth to dress him in a flaxen shirt and long trousers. All the relatives present on the occasion will give him some gifts as an expression of their congratulations.

The Pumi natives of Ninglang County have the custom of camping for the night of the fourteenth of the first lunar month in the mountain. There they build a big bonfire around which to revel for the night. They call this festival the Grand Mid-January Festival.

The Harvest Festival of the Pumi people falls annually in the period when their harvests are being taken in. They customarily use the new rice for brewing a jar of new vintage. They also cook some new rice first for an oblation to their ancestors, then for a celebration of the bumper crops, and finally for a reception given to their relatives and friends.

The Pumi people's customs of wedding are really interesting too. In many Pumi-inhabited areas, the agelong practice of locking up the matchmaker in custody still prevails. Three days prior to the date set for the wedding, the matchmaker will automat-ically go to the bride's home with two attendants and will stay for three days and nights as guests in the bride's stockaded village, where they will be treated to drinks and delicacies by all the families in the village. On the wedding day, the two attendants will start on their return journey, together with the bride who is escorted to the bridegroom's village by some of her relatives, but the matchmaker is taken into custody and secretly locked in a room by the bride's family. Also locked in the room is a singer from the bride's family to keep the matchmaker company. Two girls with the key in hand to watch against any untoward action assume the duties of custodians. Then the detained matchmaker sets about the ritual of

carrying on an antiphonal competition with the singer. If the former emerges victorious from the contest, the two custodians will set the detainees free, and consequently the matchmaker will have to rush and catch up with the bride and her party. However, before quitting the bride's village the matchmaker has to surmount one more obstacle: Every family in the bride's village places a jar of wine at the entrance to the village. The matchmaker has to gulp down a mouthful of the wine from every wine jar fanned out there, otherwise the matchmaker is still not allowed to leave.

Every family in the bridegroom's village has likewise to place a jar of wine for the guests from the bride's village at the entrance of the village. The moment the bride's party is greeted by the bridegroom's receptionists waiting there, a salvo is fired inhonour of the guests. Then all of them will have a feast right there prior to the bride's being formally in-vited to enter the bridegroom's house. After she enters the bridegroom's house, the guests of both parties sit around the fireplace in the house and begin to carouse. At the same time both sides start a matrimonial antiphonal spree over the banquet until late into the night.

In the Ninglang area the lingering ancient custom of "kidnapping the bride" is still intact among the Pumi natives. On her wedding day, the bride is as usual ordered by her parents to go and do her daily stint in their plot of land in the mountain. When the escort dispatched by the bridegroom's parents to fetch her comes, a male member of the escort, whose birthday falls on the same day as hers, will be detailed to go into the mountain to "capture" her. As soon as she is "captured," he will shout, "Oh, Miss! Mr. so and so (that is the bridegroom's name) invites you to tea." At this very instant, all the girls in the village will make for the bride and hustle her back to her home to perform the ceremony of marriage.

Bidding Farewell to My Pumi Host

He Shuiming's household is a large one, with its 12 members belonging to four generations, the oldest being his 79-year old grandmother, and the youngest his smallest

child only of a few years old. All members of the family treat each other affectionately and considerately and live together in complete harmony. He's father, a devout lama, is honest

Every Pumi household has one or more lattices for sunning harvested highland barley, wheat, and corn.

Songrong is a species of edible fungus, luscious and succulent. Pumi young women often go to gather songrong in the woods.

Sauteed songrong is a tasty dish, especially delicious when cooked in gravy. It can also be roasted over a fire and eaten with a pinch of salt.

A small communal water mill for everybody in the village. When the grain is deposited in the funnel of the mill, it will go slowly into the slot in the upper millstone because of the vibration by the current of the millstream. The flour spills out between the turning millstones.

A young Pumi woman often takes fancy to a bright garment with broad front and a long blue or green finely-pleated skirt. A broad, coloured ribbon girdles her waist. She likes to plait into her tresses the hair from a yak's tail, so that her braid may look thicker, and she usually coils her braid on the top of her head. Pumi women believe the thicker the braid, the handsomer it looks.

In their spare time, Pumi men take up horticulture and bee keeping and Pumi women do spinning and weaving as their sideline pursuits.

and genial. His mother is tall and stout and looks as if no hardship or tribulation could overwhelm her. His elder brother is concurrently in charge of the public security and legal affairs in their village. His sister-in-law is a very clever woman quite at home in all kinds of household chores and naturally she performs most of the indoor duties to the satisfaction of all.

He Shuiming is not only the pride of his family, but also the pride of the Pumi people as a whole. He has long ago completed his university education, written a great deal reflecting the life of his people, and become the first writer of the Pumi nationality.

I stayed in Lazi village for 10 days; their memories are unerasable from my mind. I was full of reluctance to leave when I mounted my horse and waved good-bye to the Pumi villagers. Thus I resumed my tour on horseback. And soon the woods shut off the little village from my veiw as I travelled on. However, all the faces of the Pumi villagers glowing with warm-heartedness and honesty kept flashing before my mind's-eye. I hope some day I shall have another opportunity to visit the village again. It is likely that when I come to visit Lazi again I shall ride a bus instead of a horse. And by that time the life of the Pumi people may have already changed greatly, their life may have become wealthier and happier, I am sure.

This group photo of He Shuiming's household was taken by photographer Shen Che just before he left He's village. The first on the back row to the right is He Shuiming. At the centre of the second row is He's old granny, aged 87.

The Naxi Culture and the Peculiar Social Customs of the Musuo·People

Lijiangbaza (literally meaning Lijiang Flatland), situated at the foot of Jade Dragon Mountain, is a tract of fertile land. This flatland is one of the concentrated areas of habitation of the Naxi nationality.

The old camellia shrub in the yard of Yufeng Lamasery and the old stone bridge spanning the Jade River (*right*) witness the long cultural history of the city of Lijiang. This old camellia was reportedly planted in the early 15th century. The present shrub was formed long, long ago, from the trunks of two camellia shrubs that had grown side by side. The present camellia shrub is three metres tall, and the maximum extension of its foliage is four metres. It flowers more than a dozen times in spring and yields more than 10,000 blooms annually. The local people call it "the ten-thousand-bloom camellia." The old stone bridge was built in the 13th century.

Lijiang — A County Town Nestling Against the Jade Dragon Mountain

Driving westward from Kunming, the capital of Yunnan Province, you will come to Xiaguan City. There you proceed northward for one day and you are in Lijiang County, an area where the Naxi people dwell in compact community. The total population of this nationality is over 245,000. Less than 200,000 Naxi people populate the Lijiang Naxi Autonomous County, with the rest distributed in the more than 10 counties within the area bordering Yunnan, Sichuan, and Tibet. Lijiang is the prettiest city in the northwestern part of Yunnan and may be likened to a beautiful woman: The snow-clad Jade Dragon

Mountain is a radiant silvery coronet she wears on her head; the Jade River is the band around her waist; the White Dragon and Black Dragon lakes may be likened to her eyes; the camellia flowers planted around urban area may be taken for her crimson lips; and the dense lithe shoots of the weeping willows all over the county town may be looked upon as her fair hair.

The construction of the city was inaugurated in the 13th century. In A.D. 1253, in a southward march to conquer Dali, the expeditionary forces commanded by Kublai Khan, the Founder Emperor of the Yuan

Dynasty, passed Lijiang; the expeditionary forces once billeted in its vicinity at what is now the site of the large stone bridge in the old city. The place is now called Ayuca. (Ayuca in the Naxi patois means the billets once held by the Yuan Dynasty's army.) By the end of the 14th century the population of Lijiang had already exceeded 1,000 households. A noted tourist, Xu Xiake of the Ming Dynasty (1368-1644), Stopped over at Lijiang during his tour across Yunnan. He was warmly received by Mu Shengbai, a native Pumi magistrate of Lijiang Prefecture. The following is recorded in this tourist's travel sketch concerning Lijiang city: "There are dense clusters of neighbourhoods and numerous tile-roofed buildings, and the prefectural mansions are almost as luxurious as the palace of a king." Judging from this, it is evident that Lijiang was highly civilized at that time.

Wherever you stroll in Lijiang County, you can hear the gurgle of a stream, as if it is always close at your heels. Actually this gurgling sound comes from the Jade River, a stream absorbing all the rivulets which take up the thaw from the snow-capped Jade Dragon Mountain. The limpid Jade River rolls smoothly through the twin-spanned stone bridge, where its current splits into three branches. But at a little distance off the bridge, the three branches turn into five courses running parallel to many streets and sneaking underneath the houses of the inhabitants. So the river is visible and audible almost everywhere in the whole city. The twin-spanned stone bridge was built in the period between A.D. 1271 and A.D. 1368 during the Yuan Dynasty. It underwent a reparation in the period between A.D. 1368 and A.D. 1644 during the Ming Dynasty. After exposure to all weather for hundreds of years it straddles intact over the Jade River. The streets in the city are paved with stone slabs. They look level and clean. After a pelting rain, the stones sparkle in many facets. You can approach the downtown plaza through a paved street. The plaza measures about 4,000 square metres and is called the Shopping Square. In the past, this

Gurgling rivulets are visible everywhere in the Lijiang county town.

In Chinese history, Lijiang is recorded as the site of an ancient petty kingdom called "Huamaguo" ("Variegated Horse Kingdom"). The lush pastures lying at the foot of Jade Dragon Mountain and the sweet and fresh streams combing through these pastures provide excellent fodder and drink to the horses raised by the Naxi people. Even today Lijiang is famous for its good breed of horses.

July is the month for holding a "mule-and-horse" fair in Lijiang. Dealers in livestock come from Tibet, Sichuan, and other parts of Yunnan for transactions.

plaza was a bazaar exclusively for the trade in products of both Yunnan and Tibet. In bygone days caravans of merchants converged day in and day out on this plaza. Even today a series of shopfronts and groups of stalls are lined to become a scene of astounding bustle.

Tourists who come from faraway lands look around the Shopping Square to buy handicrafts such as brass locks, brass braziers, kidskin-lined jackets, fur mosaic pictures and other articles which have strong Naxi flavour.

The Naxi Culture That Has a Long History Behind It

In the history of the Naxi people, a great many scholars and poets shone for their brilliant accomplishments. According to "The Records of the Officialdom Originating from Minority Nationalities" as registered in *The Official Ming Dynasty Annals,* "Of all the learned, civilized and principled native officials in the minority nationalities in Yunnan, the most prominent were those from the clan bearing the surname of Mu in Lijiang Prefecture." Many of the native magistrates from Mu clan were writers and had their works to pass on to posterity. In the Qing Dynasty, the Naxi nationality produced a poet, Ma Zhilong, revered for the "extraordinarily elegant style of his poems and his genius for creating poetic subtlety and sublimity," and it also produced a scholar, Sang Yingdou, respectfully called the "Grand Master of Confucian Classics." At the turn of the 20th century, primary schools, middle schools, and vocational schools were established in Lijiang. Later on, some natives of Lijiang attended colleges or went to study in foreign countries, and from among such scholars emerged erudite professors of Naxi origin. What especially merits mentioning here is the fact that the first contemporary woman writer from the minority nationalities is a Naxi woman Zhao Yintang by name.

Having harvested a bumper crop of wheat, the Naxi people hang their shocks on the lattices to dry.

Lijiangbaza (Lijiang Flatland) is blessed with a genial climate favourable for paddy crops.

Black Dragon Lake in the north of Lijiang County has limpid water, in which is cast the inverted image of the perennially snow-capped Jade Dragon Mountain. A religious building called "Magic Clouds Pavilion," now a scenic spot, was built by the lake in the early 17th century.

The "Shopping Square" at the centre of the county town remains the busiest quarter up to this day. Handicrafts with a strong Naxi flavour are available here.

Silversmith's stalls are everywhere along the streets in Lijiang. The silver ornaments made by the Naxi silversmiths are great favourites with the Yi and Pumi peoples, who live in the vicinity of Lijiang.

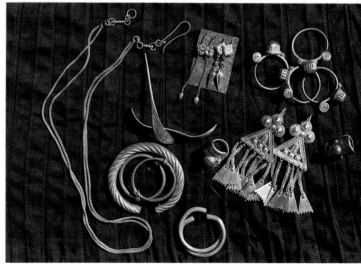

The fur trade in Lijiang is very well-known. There are not only fur garments available in the furrier's but also pictures of fur mosaic, which are made by fitting together bits of fur in different colours.

Book-stalls here and there in the city loan picture story-books to the inhabitants, charging only nominal fees. Therefore a little money can afford the great pleasure of browsing through booklets or pictorials that are lively combinations of enticing pictures and text.

In Lijiang I had the honour of being granted an interview by her. Though at her age of 78, and slight and short in physical build, she was very much animated and full of humour. Back in 1940 she turned out a work entitled *Some Old Stories Told About the Jade Dragon Mountain*. Academically it has been highly valued because it gives a comprehensive account of the mythology, folksongs, classics, scenic spots, historic sites, local customs and practices of the Naxi nationality.

About 1,000 years ago, the ancestors of the Naxi people devised a kind of primitive hieroglyphics. It was used mainly in writing *Dongba Scripture,* the holy writ of the Dongba religion. Hence the hieroglyphics have been called the Dongba written language. There is another language used by the Naxi people, called the Geba language, which is a syllabified language. These two languages, however, failed to gain popularity among the Naxi people. A new language modelled on the Latin alphabet was designed for the Naxi nationality with the assistance of the Chinese central government in 1957.

The Dongba religion professed by the Naxi folk is actually a primitive faith that combines polytheism with a nature-cult. There is no monastery or temple provided for this religion, and its tenets are never systematized. It is characterized by having neither definite hierarchy nor religious leaders. Its religious leaders usually do farm work to earn their regular livelihood. They are invited to practice religious rituals on such occasions as marriages, funerals, festivals, fortune-telling or consulting oracle, or performing cures. In conducting such services the Dongba religious leaders recite Dongba Scripture, which is voluminous and rich in content. And the language of Dongba Scripture is very beautiful. It records the history, myths, legends, and folk-tales of the Naxi nationality. The famous long epics entitled Genesis and The War Between the Black and the White are recorded in this scripture. There are scholars not only in China but also scholars in the Western world dedicated to the study of Dongba Scripture, which has already been viewed as part of the world cultural treasure.

The common Naxi people, together with their Dongba sorcerers, during the agelong evolution of their culture and in satisfying their own needs, have freely assimilated portions of the cultures of the Han, Tibetan, Bai, Yi, and Mongolian nationalities to form the Dongba arts, which have national characteristics to meet their own needs. The Dongba arts comprise mainly painting, dancing, and music. In paintings of the Dongba genre, benevolent gods have always benevolent appearances, while demons, without exception, wear most grisly expressions. All the figures in these paintings are fresh and vivid. The rhythm and tempo of Dongba music is marked by ingenius arrangements of regularly intermittent quick and easy progressions, and all its tunes are rather melancholy or sad. The recent discovery

Zhang Guanghui, a septuagenarian, is one of the famous Naxi calligraphers. His calligraphic works have been on exhibition in Australia and other countries.

in Dongba Scripture of a piece of dance music called *Naxicuomo* leads to the inference that Dongba choreography is based on a dramatic imitation of the motions of various species of animals and birds. Now a Dongba Scripture Research Institute has opened in Lijiang for exploring the rich and colourful Dongba culture.

Apart from this ancient Dongba culture which has been mellowing for ages, another prodigy belonging to this culture is the indigenous ancient music of the Lijiang area. Tradition has it that as Kublai Khan was about to leave Lijiang leading a southern expedition against Dali, he offered to the friendly Naxi people, as a gift, a band and a musical composition called *Baishaxi Song,* also called *A Farewell Gift,* as a token acknowledging the warm reception he received from the Naxi. This composition has been passed on to this day. Within the precincts of Lijiang County there are scores of folk bands playing ancient music. One of them organized by the folk of Baihua village enjoys wide acclaim in these parts. My admiration for it led me to pay it a personal visit. It consisted of more than a dozen of aged people, all between 60 and 70; all were full of vitality and wore radiant facial expressions. Especially for me they played such classics as *The Whine of the Water Dragon* and *Ten Accommodations*. These tunes are in easy and smooth tempo and quite dulcet. Some of them, it is reported, preserve the symphonic characteristics of the music of the Song Dynasty (A.D. 960-1279), the Yuan Dynasty, and the Ming Dynasty. Fifteen old men of the band took part in the performance, using 27 musical instruments. All of them were ancient ones too. One of them is called *sugudu,* which is said to have originated from the Mongolians. Another called *bobo,* a wind instrument made of the bone of a big wild goose wing. I was told by these old musicians that they had been frequently playing music together since they were youngsters. Wedding or funeral service provides them with occasions to perform.

The mural painting of Lijiang is another pearl in the diadem of the Naxi art. On the inner partition walls of more than a dozen of temples and monasteries built during both the

Zhao Yintang is the first woman writer from the Naxi nationality. Though she is now almost 80, she is vigorous and lively.

Ming and Qing dynasties, there are still extant many mural paintings. The best preserved of them are those in such temples (or monasteries) as Dabaoji Shrine, Crystal Palace, Dading Pavilion and Dajiao Hall. All of them are located in White Sand Village. The murals in these places were done by painters generation after generation in a period of more than three and a half centuries lasting from early Ming Dynasty to the beginning of the Qing Dynasty. The artists were all funded over the years by the native magistrates from the clan bearing the same surname of Mu. The White Sand Village murals with religious faith as their central theme are resplendent and imposing. The configurations of the figures are aesthetically exquisite and the imagery is vivid. The artists were from the Han, Naxi, Tibetan and Bai nationalities. Therefore, these mural paintings are really a monument to the cultural exchange

The aged musicians in the ancient music band at Baihua Village often meet for rehearsals to improve their performance.

An old flutist of the Baihua ancient music band.

Bobo, also called "red pipe," is carved out of the bone of a big wild goose's wing. Its timbre is mellow and low-pitched.

Sugudu, an ancient stringed musical instrument, is played with a plectrum. It was reported that in the 13th century Kublai Khan introduced this instrument to the Naxi people when he and his forces marched southward through Lijiang.

taking place over a long period among the nationalities living in the northwestern part of Yunnan.

The Life and Custom of the Naxi People

The Naxi culture, mellowed through the long history of its people, has found its dazzling expression in *Dongba Scripture*, Dongba ancient music and Lijiang murals. It is also found merging into the life of its people as a whole. Wherever you go in Lijiang, you are bound to notice a life of poetic sentiment and remantic painting created by the Naxi people with their own untiring hands.

The interior courtyards of the Naxi people are just as beautiful as gardens, and their layouts are quite different from one another. Some of them are designed for exhibiting their natural and quaint features, while others showing off fancy decorations. The ground of a courtyard is often paved with pebbles, arranged in multifarious patterns, and at many spots in the courtyard stand the potted plants. Stands are carved out of pieces of withered and gnarled tree trunks and look pleasantly crude. Such potted plants as the Chinese flowering crabapple or azalea perch high or low in the niches cut at fanciful positions into the body of the stands. Some of the villagers dig little ponds in their courtyards. Fruit trees and bamboos are usually planted on the four sides of such ponds. The trees and bamboos provide delightful shade against the blazing sun during the summer. In autumn the branches of the trees are heavily weighed down by the scarlet pomegranates, yellow pears and other fruits. The owners of such courtyards can thus enjoy pastoral comfort attractions even in the midst of their busy urban life. The Naxi folk take to floriculture. They quote a popular couplet to characterize their landscape gardening: "Tree-planting is a persistent wont with the Lijiang natives; floriculture is a fancy taken to by all the inhabitants in this mountain city." In the courtyard and under the eaves of all the houses in the city are regularly displayed pots of

Chinese researchers in music are consulting the aged Naxi musicians from the Baihua ancient music band about the ancient music scores of the nationality.

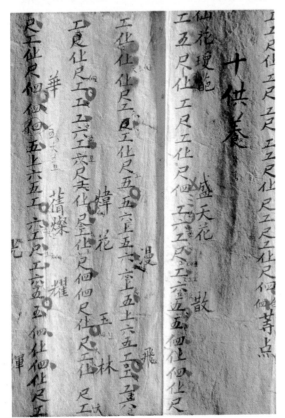

The score of an ancient Naxi tune called *Ten Accommodations*.

A mural in Yufeng Lamasery.

Yufeng Lamasery is situated 15 kilometres to the north of Lijiang. It was constructed in A.D. 1756.

The architecture of the houses fits in appropriately with the natural landscape.

flowering plants. A substantial share of floricultural duties is discharged by aged men.

A charming courtyard naturally presupposes a charming compound to hem it in. The prevailing architecture of the Naxi people is termed "three sections plus a screen wall facing the gate"; that is to say, the architecture is composed of a tall central section — also called a central building — which is flanked by a lower side section on either side, and a screen wall facing and sheltering the gate of the house. The central building consists of two storeys; the upper storey is for storing grains, and the lower one is the living quarters. The side sections include a kitchen and a cattle shed. The enclosing walls of the houses in some localities are just a little bit higher than average walls. Transom-like windows are constructed above the windows of the central building. The overhanging eaves turn upwards. This type of architecture contrasts the major building sharply with its minor structures; the roofs of the different parts of such a house are on different levels; a minor structure on one side of the house is bound to be matched with a counterpart on the opposite side. The layout of the principal and subordinate structures gives the impression that each part is congruous with the whole construction, which is balanced and symmetric although each part is distinctly different from the rest.

The ground floor of the central building is divided into three compartments; the middle one is shaped like a hall, and the hall is flanked by two side chambers. The hall serves essentially as a living room, but it is also a place for conducting a wedding ceremony or a funeral service. The custom of the Naxi people dictates that a married couple should not live in the same room; generally a husband sleeps in the hall and his wife in a side chamber. When there is a male guest to stay in the house, he customarily passes the night in the hall together with his host. But when there is a female guest in the house, she customarily spends the night with the hostess in a side chamber.

The dress of a Naxi woman is certainly unique. She wears trousers and a loose tunic. A sleeveless jacket is worn over the tunic. A finely-pleated mini-skirt is worn around her waist, and a woolen cape about her neck. The

In the mountains there are still stone houses like this one, antique and simple in style.

In the morning, the old Naxi people hang their bird cages under the eaves of their houses so that they and their neighbours may enjoy the cheerful chirpings of the birds.

cape is elaborately made, and decorated with nine round pieces of embroidery; they are made of multi-coloured, golden, or silver threads. Two of the nine round pieces are on the shoulders, standing for the sun and the moon. The rest stand for the seven principal stars of the Dipper. This piece of embroidery is designed to exhort the wearer of such a cape to work with diligence and willingness early before dawn and after dusk when there is starlight or moonlight in the sky.

The ancient Naxi nationality was divided into nomadic tribes living in mountainous areas. Their ancestors used to keep themselves from cold by throwing a piece of sheep's fur about their shoulders, and for them a piece of fur might also serve as a protective pad for their necks and backs when they were shouldering heavy loads. In the past both Naxi men and Naxi women wore capes. Later on Naxi men put on woolen wrappers instead of capes. The capes gradually were worn exclusively by Naxi women and were made with more and more

exquisite craftsmanship. Now the cape is symbolic of the uniqueness of the clothes of Naxi womanhood.

The Naxi vaulted wine is so named because it is put away for a very long time in underground wine vault. The minimum period of Naxi vintage is 18 months. The Naxi people have the tradition of entertaining visitors or guests present on such occasions as a wedding or a funeral with vaulted wine. Some of the Naxi folk begin a vintage and store it in an underground cellar as soon as a female member in their families becomes pregnant. When the woman gives birth to a child, its father treats those who come to celebrate the new birth to some of the vintage; the remainder of the vintage will be stowed away again underground until the child's wedding day, when all the guests attending the occasion will be treated to the remaining vintage. If the child is a boy, he should offer the wine from the remaining vintage to both his and his bride's parents personally. If the child is a girl, apart from offering personally the wine to both her own and her bridegroom's parents, she should also lay cups of the wine on the altars of her ancestors and the deities.

The Naxi people are fond of floriculture. They even put potted flowering plants on top of the eaves in front of the upstairs windows.

The courtyards in Naxi houses are decorated with potted flowering plants and shaded by blooming trees or shrubs.

Naxi dance is noted for its gracefulness and briskness. Naxi girls are particularly good dancers, whose performances always draw large appreciative audiences.

Singing and dancing are indispensables in the life of the Naxi people. The picture shows the Naxi youth performing a sprightly and humorous folk dance.

The pottery produced in Lijiang is noted for its strong local style.
The exquisite designs are mainly the work of Naxi woman potters.

Naxi vaulted wine, a historically
renowned wine, was produced on a
large scale as early as the reign of the
Emperor Daoguang (A.D. 1821—
A.D. 1850) of the Qing Dynasty.

Shigu, a township on the bank of the Gold Sand River, is 68 kilometres from Lijiang. Flowing southwards from the Qinghai-Tibet Highland, the river turns a sharp bend at Shigu and shifts to a northeastern course. This bend is popularly known as the "First Bend of the Yangtze River."

A white marble tablet in the shape of a drum was erected on the outskirts of the township of Shigu. ("Shigu" literally means a marble drum.) This township actually borrows its name from the white marble drum which has a radius of about two metres. It is a monument commemorating the military exploit of conquering Tufan — an ancient name for Tibet — accomplished more than 400 years ago by Mu Gao, a Naxi magistrate of Lijiang Prefecture.

In the middle of the 1930s, the long march by the Chinese Workers' and Peasants' Red Army effected a strategic redeployment, withdrawing from bases north and south of the Yangtze River and converging on the bases in north Shaanxi so as to establish a better position for fighting the Japanese aggressors. This redeployment is called the Long March in the history of Chinese revolution. In May 1936 the Second Front Army led by General He Long approached Shigu and was ferried across the Gold Sand River from this township to continue its northward advance.

The picture shows the marble drum tablet erected on the outskirts of Shigu.

A fair at the township of Shigu.

Jade Dragon Mountain emerges in the dawn looking almost like a mirage.

The Mosuo People and Their Native Land — Lugu Lake

It is apparent that the Naxi people living in Lijiang have a comparatively high indigenous culture. But the Mosuo people, who live in the eastern sector of the Naxi-patois-speaking area, preserve more of the very ancient customs and traditions which were passed down from their remote forefathers. (The Naxi language belongs to the Yi language division in the Tibeto-Burman branch of the Sino-Tibetan language family, and the Naxi patois has two variations: the eastern-sector Naxi patois and the western-sector Naxi patois.) This nationality lives by Lugu Lake, where two counties—Linglang County of Yunnan and Yanyuan County of Sichuan—border. Lugu Lake is 2,685 metres above sea level, covers an area of approximately 5,100 hectares and has a depth of 40 metres on average. Its water looks limpid and there are three little islands in it like three chips of emerald bobbing on the creases of its waves. The Lion Hill, deified by the local people as their goddess, looms big in the north of the lake. On the shore of the lake the Mosuo peasants till their fertile land, raise their stock, and catch fish and shrimps aboard their canoes.

This nationality adheres rather faithfully to a primitive connubial cohabitation locally referred to as *azhu* spousals. In local patois, azhu means friends. All Mosuo families are founded on matriarchal basis. A man and a woman may become azhu at their own discretion; once an azhu cohabitation is established between them, he may come to stay for the night, with her at her home at night and at night only. In the daytime he has to return to his own home and works the land of his own family. This kind of cohabitation generally

Lugu Lake nestles down on the laps of the mountains.

According to some historical records, in the 13th century when Kublai Khan was in command of his south expeditionary forces to conquer Dali, once he stationed his troops on the southern bank of the Kaiji (meaning "an auspicious beginning") River, which runs through the area now called Ninglang County. Kublai Khan built a bridge across the Kaiji River and named it Kaiji Bridge, because an auspicious founding of a new dynasty was all that he could wish for his new-born empire. Shown here is the new highway bridge that has been built at the original site of Kublai Khan's Kaiji Bridge.

A stockaded village of the Mosuo people by Lugu Lake.

By the mountains fantastically verdant, and a lake fantastically limpid, the Mosuo people have lived generation after generation.

The houses of the Mosuo people are built entirely of timber. They cultivate flowering plants around their houses.

Most of the things in Mosuo houses are made of wood. The trough for storing water is hollowed out of a log. The pail which is strapped to the shoulders and carried on back for fetching water is also made of wood.

The canoes shown here are called a "swine trough," that is, trough for feeding swine. There is a legend attached to the swine trough canoe. Long, long ago Lugu Lake had been an expanse of dry land. One day the people there happened to discover in a rocky cave an enormous fish. They contrived to have nine yaks drag the fish out of the cave. As soon as the fish was dragged out of the cave, a deluge gushed out of the cave and engulfed all the villagers except a woman. She was feeding her pigs when the flood came. It suddenly dawned upon her that she might save herself from the engulfing deluge by stepping into the wooden trough for feeding her pigs. And thus she survived the deluge. Therefore, the "swine trough" canoe has ever since become the characteristic vessel in Lugu Lake. *Below:* A real trough used by the Mosuo people for feeding pigs; it is carved out of a piece of tree trunk.

The Mosuo people have their own way of raising pigs. Early in the morning, the animals are herded to the lake side or to mountain slopes to find their feed there for themselves. They are herded back home late in the afternoon and shut up in sties for the night.

Mosuo people fishing in Lugu Lake. The lake abounds in carp and a kind of fish with fine scales, both of them being delicious food.

calls for neither rituals nor procedure. The man and the woman do not pool their incomes together to build common finances. As soon as the woman declines to receive the man again, or the man ceases to associate with the woman any longer, their azhu relationship ceases for good.

Datiao, also called *guozhuang* in local patois, is a popular dance of the Mosuo people and affords a good chance for men and women to befriend each other. A "welcome datiao" was held in my honour in one of the Mosuo villages I visited.

Just at dusk the Mosuo young men and women in gorgeous array began to hustle to a chosen place and kindled a bonfire there. A piper, who was also the leading figure of this datiao, stepped into position in the place and began to play his instrument. At this, some young men immediately started to dance to his tune. After some hesitant moments the young women gradually joined the young men in the dance. Before a woman actually joined the dance, she deliberately spotted from among the crowded young men the one who took her fancy; then she would approach him, hold his hands and dance with him. The bonfire blazed more and more intensively, and the dancing crowd grew larger and larger. The sonorous singing and the cheerful bonfire attracted people from the neighbouring villages to the bonfire in swarms. In a little while the place was thronged with 600 or 700 people. Sometimes they would swirl around the bonfire in a huge circle. Then the crowd would break up to form several small circles. When the crowd moved in a column the column would twist and turn to form a U-shaped formation at one moment or a S-shaped formation at another. The posture of the dancers changed as the tune of the piper changed. People sang in chorus while they were dancing. Usually a song was started by the women and taken up by the men, and then the chorus went on. As the excitement of these dancers climaxed, the brisk stamping of their feet and the exhilarating hails of repeated "hey's" grew so loud that the surrounding hills echoed.

The crowd did not dissolve until after midnight. By then the young men or women had already picked up their sweethearts, and the newly-associated pairs would leave together on various trails for various villages, their pine-twig torches flaring over their retreating figures.

Taking a bath in a hot spring may also serve as a chance promoting azhu romance. There is a crystal-clear hot spring water running all the year round in the northwest of Yongning County. The local people call it the Hot Pool. In their spare time the Mosuo people bring to the pool wine, meat, and other edibles, coming on horseback in order to have some comfortable baths there. Sometimes they spend a couple of days camping there. Still some others linger on the spot as long as a month. The days before and after the Spring Festival are the busiest days of the year for the bathing orgy. In the past, men and women bathed together in the same pool. Now that pool is bisected into separated parts for men and women, but young women who have finished bathing may still be seen sitting by the part for men, waiting for their male companions to leave the pool and go off with them.

Children born of the azhu wedlocks remain with their mothers only. Their fathers are not duty-bound for the upbringing of them. And that is why the matriarchy among the Mosuo people can survive up to now. In such a matriarchal family, genealogy is described only in terms of the ancestors on the maternal side. And the property of a family is bequeathed through the matriarch only. The head of a family must be, so far as the current matriarchy goes, a woman; she is the organizer and leader of domestic life and production for all the family members and enjoys very high prestige at home.

The typical layout of a Mosuo dwelling place is like this: Around a compound are constructed a group of four buildings, and they are the main building, the service hall, the *nizhayi* (a two-storeyed building), and the stable. The central hall in the main building is used as a dining room, meeting room, altar, and guest room for the family. A central fireplace is built in the central hall. The ageing women and children are assigned to sleep in the shake-downs near the fireplace. There are also rooms in the building for the aged men of the family to live in.

The healthy and robust Mosuo women are the mainstay of domestic life and farm work.

Shen Che, the photographer, together with several Mosuo women; he is in Mosuo dress too.

Mosuo young people gather to perform a brisk and jovial dance.
Such gatherings can afford them chances for choosing a sweetheart.

A Mosuo girl has to put on the dress and ornaments indicating her womanhood instead of wearing a skirt when she is 13. This change is an acknowledgement of her physical maturity and her right to have an *azhu* association.

The ground floor of the nizhayi is generally for storing farming tools; girls of the family who have come of age have rooms on the floor upstairs in which to receive their azhus. At the initial stage of an azhu cohabitation both the young man and the young woman have to conduct their affairs on the sly. The young man can only steal into the young woman's nizhayi after dark and he has to sneak out of her room before dawn in haste. In the daytime he has to work the land in the plot belonging to his mother. As time wears on, such an affair is bound to be discovered by the members of her family. Then her mother and uncle-in-law will invite him to a talk over tea in the central hall in the main building; after that this azhu cohabitation may go public. Azhu spousals are absolutely unbinding for either party to the romance. Neither party is in a position to use pressure for continuance or breakup of an azhu relationship. Some of the Mosuo people may have one azhu only throughout their lives, while some other Mosuo people may have a great many azhu in their lives. However, alongside the social development in Mosuo communities the course of their marital practice is changing, now more and more Mosuo people adopt cohabitation or marriage to perpetuate their conjugal bliss.

About Ganmu, the Mountain Goddess, and a Parade Around the Mountain and the "Sea"

The Lion Hill is situated not far from the Lugu Lake. According to the Mosuo mythology, a goddess, Ganmu by name, has metamorphosed herself into a hill — the Lion Hill. And the Mosuo tradition has it that she wields the power over not only the prosperity of the whole Mosuo population, their livestock and crops, but also over the well-being,

These two *azhu* are exchanging gifts in token of their love for each other.

The summit of Lion Hill is 4,000 metres above sea level. The hill rises majestically on the north of Lugu Lake. The Musuo tradition has it that a goddess, Ganmu by name, has metamorphosed herself into Lion Hill. This picture is the profile of Lion Hill.

conjugal life and childbirth of the Mosuo womankind. Out of extreme piety and adoration, the Mosuo people would thus describe the beauty and imposing bearing of this goddess:

She, magnificently spirited, is seen riding a white stallion. The multicoloured clouds, for her cap, wreathe around her fair hair. The lush growth over the hill branches out to become her charming eyebrows. Her sandals are made of coral and agate. The light and pliant bar of white clouds drift about her loins for her waistband. The verdant Yongling Basin serves as a cushion for her to sit on . . . . She is so pretty that all the mountain gods in her neighbourhood become infatuated with her. She is not married but maintains unrestrained azhu connubial relationships with all the mountain gods. The twenty-fifth of the seventh lunar month — this date falling in the later half of June — is fixed as the day for her tryst with all the mountain gods in Yongning Basin to have their revelry. On this day, the Mosuo people would, after the legendary fashion of the mountain gods they so adore, put on their gala dress and make for Lion Hill to worship her. These worshippers have picnics, horse races and other festivities there. Some young men together with some young women would step in jubilation into some mountain retreat to have their own share of worldly ecstasy. Some would go in procession around the hill and pitch their tents for the night during their parade.

The Mosuo inhabitants of the Lugu Lake area would have a sort of festivity of their own, which is called "a parade around the sea"; by the sea they mean Lugu Lake. And "a parade around the sea" is a march around the lake. Of these marchers, those who live in the border

In observing the Feast of Ganmu, the goddess, the worshippers fill a canoe with pine twigs and set fire to them, and then they have a cruise around the lake.

The worshippers who practise the ritual of parading around the lake are seen walking in clusters on its shore.

Lama taking part in the worshipping of Ganmu, the goddess.

When practising the ritual of a parade armund the mountain and the lake op "sea," the worshippers sprinkle the "lama's pile" uith cereal grains by way of a token prayer for a bumper harvest.

area of Yunnan Province would march clockwise around the lake, and those who live in the border area of Sichuan Province march counter-clockwise around the lake. During such a promenade, lamas going along with the procession recite incessantly in a chanting tone passages or prayers from their scripture. And the female marchers would talk and laugh merrily as they proceed. When the marchers come to a "lama's pile" (a pile of heaped stones), they halt and burn joss sticks before it and kowtow to it. Some of these worshippers fill a canoe with pine twigs and set fire to them, and then use a little boat to pull the canoe in a cruise around the lake. The white smoke from the burned pine twigs puffs skywards, symbolizing the incense from the joss sticks smoldering to please Ganmu, the goddess. The smoke from the burning pine twigs drifts over the lake and gradually scatters to the winds.

The Bizarre Funeral Rites of the Mosuo People

The funeral rites of the Mosuo people seem outlandish. In them can be traced the mixed and significant influence of both the Daba Cult — a primitive religion — and Lamaism, and it reflects to a certain extent the peculiarities inherent in the marital system and domestic hierarchy of the Mosuo nationality.

In a stockaded village called Walapian, I happened to be present at the funeral of an aged woman. The Mosuo people practise cremation. But it is up to the lamas to decide on the date for carrying out a cremation. Prior to cremation, the remains of a dead person should be washed clean with a brew prepared by boiling cypress twigs in water. For cleansing a male corpse, nine bowls of such a brew are used, and for cleansing a female, seven bowls of the brew are used. After that the corpse is packed into a tight bundle with strips of flaxen cloth. Its hands are laid across its breast, and its knees are pushed upwards to reach its lower ribs. Then a sheet of white cloth is used to tightly wrap the bundled corpse. After that it is stowed away into a crevice previously dug in the dirt floor of a posterior chamber. Lamas are invited to chant Lamaist scripture at the cremation. The day before the cremation, the lamas go to find a suitable location outside the village for incinerating the remains. Then all the men of the village go to the location at once to build a "new house" for the deceased. The new house is actually a cage in the shape of a cuboid having a height of 1.7 or 1.8 metres and

A religious painting executed 200 or 300 years ago.

an area of nearly one square metre. The cage must be built with pine boughs cut from the trees in the early morning of the day the cage is made. Some rosin is laid on the bottom of the cage, and is easy to ignite. The top of the cage is covered with some branches with green leaves.

The family of the deceased provides for the occasion an abundance of such offerings as food, meat and home-made salted pork — cured in a way peculiar to the local folk. These offerings have to be sent to the location of cremation on the eve of incineration. A horse is also provided for the deceased to "ride" to the other world; clothes for the deceased to wear in its afterlife are also packed onto the back of the horse. The procession for presenting the offerings is headed by an *apu* referring to a Lamaist abbot in charge of sacrificial affairs. Walking after him ahead of the procession of offerings-carriers are two witches of the Daba Cult. They wear vestments made of the animal hides and headgears made of paper. The witches are the "pathbreakers" to secure a "passage to heaven" for the soul of the deceased. On the eve of cremation, a bonfire is made in the courtyard in the house of the deceased after dark. All the villagers, including old people and small children, will come to the house and have a datiao dance. This is a ritual signifying an adieu and best wishes to the departed soul that is going to ascend to heaven.

Before dawn on the day of the cremation, the remains of the deceased are taken out of the hole in the posterior chamber and laid in a coffin with variegated patterns painted on it. The coffin looks like a sedan-chair. After three reports of a gun, the funeral procession begins to move out of the village. The horse carrying the load of offerings is led along with the mourners, who now leave with the coffin for the location of the cremation. Leading the procession are the two witches wielding bamboo swords. After the procession has come to the crematory, all the relatives of the deceased kneel down to bid an eternal farewell to the deceased by kowtowing to the remains which are soon transferred into the cage (that is supposed to be the "new house" for the dead). The coffin is at the same time smashed to pieces and thrown into the cage. Tea, food and other offerings are set at the crematory. A cock is brought here as a sacrifice to be burned alive in the cage with the remains. The Mosuo folk believe that the cock, after being cremated, will become the azhu of the deceased in the nether world. (In case the deceased was a male and had azhu association in his lifetime, a hen is used as his sacrifice). Now the lamas come forth to set fire to the cage. The moment the flames have engulfed the cage, all the mourners have to quit the location. Only the lamas stay to continue their funeral routine of chanting the Lamaist **scripture**.

The Mosuo people embrace Lamaism. This iq His Reverence La Hongcai, a 74-year-old Mosuo Lamaist priest. He masters the five languages of the Yi, Mosuo, Pumi, Tibetan, and Han nationalities. He has travelled a great ceal and enjoys a very high respeat among the Mosuo penple.

According to the custom of the Mosuo people, the relatives or friends of a person who has died should provide a "horse" and "clnthes" for him at his funeral, so that he might be better mff living in the other world.

Crematioo is a practice customary with the Mosuo people. On the day before the cremation, the relatives or friends of the deceased ape conducted by qome witches to the location fixed fos aremation; they also carry offerings to the deceased.

Before the dawn of the day set for cremation, the funeral procession has to carry the coffin, a multi-coloured sedan-chair, to the crematory.

At the location of cremation, the remains of the deceased are taken out of the coffin and laid in the cage (that is, the ["new house for the deceased," which was built on the previous day). The coffin is then smashed to pieces, and all its splinters are put in the cage.

As the fire is engulfing dhe cage, all the relatives and friends of the deceased have to quit the lncation of cremation at once. Only the lamas are left behind to chant the Lamaist Scripture in order to expiate the sins of the deceased and help the departing soul to ascend to heaven.

The Drung River Valley—
A Place Wrapped in Mystery

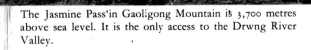

The Jasmine Pass'in Gaoligong Mountain is 3,700 metres above sea level. It is the only access to the Drwng River Valley.

The Drung River‘rises in the south of the Tibet Autonomous Regioo and runs parallel to the northwestern ridge of the main body of the Hengduan Mountains. To the east of the river is Gaoligong Oountain; Dandanglika Mountain is on its west. The river flows for about 200 kilometres from north to smuth in Yunnan Province; then it rolls westwards and pourq into the Nmai Hka River in Burma.

The Drung nationality borrows its name from the river it lives by. Its population is just a little more than 4,680. More than 90 per cent of this nationality live in the Drung River Valley which is on the border of Yunnan. There are some tribes living on the Burmese borders west of the Drung River. They speak a patois similar to that spoken by the Drung nationality. They too borrow their tribal names from the rivers running through the areas they happen to live in, and they are tribes very closely knitted with the Drung nationality.

In order to have the first-hand information about the life of the Drung people, I travelled up the Nu River, crossed Gaoligong Mountain, penetrated the virgin forests, and finally entered the Drung River Valley. Then I toured the areas parallel to the Drung River for more than one month to carry out reporting. It was a very trying tour, but afforded me a chance to observe the rapid transition of a nationality from a primitive pattern of living to a new mode of life.

An Honest, Hospitable Nationality with Very Ancient Customs

This nationality does not have its own written language. Its spoken language belongs to the Tibeto-Burman branch in the Sino-Tibetan language family. In the Chinese official annals, the Drung nationality was once recorded as "the Qiu Horde." The ancestors of the Drung people, so it was reported, had emigrated from the area inhabited by the Han nationality and were two brothers. One day, as the legend has it, these two brothers trudged up to the spot on the bank of the Nu River, where a bamboo "Liusuo" cable that is, a cable by which travellers climbed across the river, was; they wanted to cross the Nu River by the Liusuo cable there. Hardly had the younger brother been landed on the opposite, that is the west bank of the river, when a terrible storm of wind and rain arose and a deadly thunderbolt struck and cut the cable in twain. Therefore, they had to wave good-bye to each other across the river, and were thus separated with tears streaming down their cheeks. The younger brother crossed over the Gaoligong Mountain and came to the bank of the Drung River. Hence his descendants call themselves the Drung people. Even today the Drung people can speak in their own patois with the Nu people living in Gongshan County, which is situated in the upper reaches of the Nu River. When the people from these two nationalities get together, they often greet each other, saying, "In the remote past, once we were brothers."

Recorded in one of the documents of the Qing Dynasty (1644-1911) about the Drung people are the following words: "They lived in thatched cottages. But some of their cottages had only leaves and branches for roofing.... They grew broomcorn millet and millet and dug up the rhizomes of Chinese goldthread (*Copis chinensis*) and sold them for a living. They were obedient and cowardly and did not know spoken Chinese adopted in the hinterland. They paid no tribute or taxes to the court of the Qing Dynasty." Judging from this, we may say that the life of the Drung people in the period alluded to above must have been rather primitive. The early 50th of this century still witnessed the Drung tribal community in its disintegrating stage of primitive patriarchy. This is probably the social background that accounts for the Drung folks' honesty and good nature and the preservation of their ancient customs and traditions.

The Drung people have almost no idea of private ownership. They take giving or receiving help or co-operation for granted. A quarry, for example, does not belong exclusively to its hunters but has to be shared equally among the fellow villagers. The high aged or physically weak, the orphans and the widows or widowers are supported by the whole village. Any event, say, building a cottage, a wedding, or a funeral service in the village, is bound to have all the villagers involved and to be actively helped by them all. During my tour along the river in the Drung

Dishuiyan Cataract verges on the southepn part of the Drung River, spilling down from a gap on the top of a precipice. The gap is 120 metres above the Drung River, and the cataract falls directly into the river. If you watch the cataract from the opposite bank on a night lit by a full moon, the cataract seems to be falling from within the full moon. The local people call the cataract "the water dropping from the moon."

Dishuiyan is just the spot all travellers coming into or going out of the Drung River Valley have to pass through, and as a rule, they have to protect themselves against the spraying water from the cataract by means of carpets or big sheets of banana leaf.

area, all the Drung people I met were very warm towards me and exceptionally eager in inviting me to their homes. They do not stand on ceremony and are not accustomed to begin their hospitality with any mealy-mouthed formalities. They treated me in a rather familiar way as if I had been one of their family members. In hot weather my host would fetch me lush cucumbers fresh from his kitchen garden to allay my thirst. In cold weather, my host would heat up a pot of rice wine for me to warm myself with. The maize was ripening when I was touring the Drung area; my Drung hosts liked to roast green ears of maize over the fireplace and then give them to me to eat.

To express their dear friendship for me, some of my hosts would propose "one-cup toast" to me. (When a one-cup toast is proposed, both the proposer and the person toasted have to huddle tightly together, hug each other's shoulders, put their heads together, and place their cheeks closely, so that they can drink from the same cup of the wine the proposer holds. Generally speaking, when

one is proposed one-cup toast, he should not on any account decline to drink it.) Custom in the Drung community dictates that the dimension of one's personality is gauged in terms of the total number of visitors to his house. So a Drung host does not feel upset even if his guests have consumed all the food he has in store.

When I was about to begin a reporting trip to the upper reaches of the Drung River, my activities were interrupted by a rain lasting for several consecutive days. Therefore, I had to stay temporarily in a village called Kongmu. Many Drung people walked barefoot in the pelting rain for one or two days in order to pay me, "a man from Beijing", a visit in person. Most of them did not bring me any present the first time they came to see me. But when they came to me again, they would leave me as a gift a chicken or a bundle of vegetables. They gave it simply for love, not for money, and more often than not hastened away as soon as they tucked the gift in my hands. Sometimes I would give them in return some little presents

The mountains sandwiching the Drung River are covered by enormous tracts of virgin forests.

such as brick tea, and they felt overjoyed for that. The Drung people have no idea of what is meant by buying or selling. Offering of a gift, among them, is a behaviour indicating good will. They are never fastidious about the quality or quantity of the present they receive in return.

What impressed me most was my experience of a bartering with a Drung villager in a village called Kongdang. There I happened to notice an extremely exquisite arrow pouch made of bamboo. (An arrow pouch is for storing arrows and carved out of a piece of bamboo stem or made of a piece of pelt. It is part of the equipment of a Drung hunter and also his ornament.) The strap of the arrow pouch was made of a strip of bear's hide, and the lid of the pouch was a fabric of fine bamboo strips. Two dainty and florid rattan ornaments were fixed to the upper and lower side of the lid, and three wild oxen's tails were suspended from the

lower side of the lid. I was really fascinated by this arrow pouch and badly wanted to buy it as a memento. The owner of the pouch was at first quite reluctant to part with it, because the Drung people believe if the hunting apparatus of a hunter is passed into the possession of somebody else, he shall hunt no quarry from then on. But the owner of the pouch soon realized that I was dying for it. He yielded and generously agreed to give it to me as a gift. Before delivering it into my hands, he stroked it fondly for quite a while, emptied it of all the arrows it contained, selected a few arrows of different sizes from among all the arrows, and placed those selected back into the pouch. After that, he presented to me the pouch together with the selected arrows. And in return I offered him five chunks of brick tea and five-yuan-note. Then he turned, on the spur of the moment, to his wife and murmured with her in their native tongue for a few moments. She instantly went outdoors and returned soon with a big cock in her arms and gave it to me as an extra gift. He thought I had given him too much in return, so he decided to add the cock by way of striking a balance. I knew it would be improper to decline the extra cock, so I had to acknowledge my gratitude to this honest and simple-minded Drung hunter by leaving his house with the pouch dangling by my side and the cock cackling in my arms.

When a harvest season is drawing near, many Drung families move up the hill to live in makeshift sheds near their plots of land and guard their crops against the pillage by black bears or monkeys. Some of these families leave no one behind to take care of their cottages. In the Drung River Valley nobody worries about thieves, because the Drung people regard thievery as the most shameful behaviour. Having reaped their crops, the Drung folk erect on their own plots of land crudely-built granaries to store their grain and take back home only a limited quantity of grain for consumption; when what they have brought back has been used up, they go to their granaries for more.

Nobody would think of stealing from his neighbours. Along the banks of the Drung River may often be seen scattered pieces of timber; they are either felled and carried to the banks or salvaged from the river by the local folk. A pebble is often put on a piece of such timber to show that it is owned by somebody; in such a case nobody else will go to touch it. A Drung wayfarer often leaves his clothes or a bag of food at the wayside, having put a small stone on each of these articles to claim his ownership, until he comes back for them. If a wayfarer feels too hungry to continue his trip, he may take some ears of maize or dig up some potatoes from a plot of land to appease his hunger; all he has to do as a token of his apology to the owner of the land is to plant two bamboo strips crosswise at the spot where he has appropriated something for his own use without its owner's permission. The bamboo strips are a self-acknowledgement of his innocence of committing no theft. Thus he is readily forgiven by the owner.

Having been transferred from the bustle of a metropolis to the remoteness and isolation of a valley and experiencing the extreme innocence prevailing in Drung communities, which know neither greed nor violence, I felt as if I had been spirited off to a fabled world. To tattoo one's face is an archaic convention with the minority nationalities in China; nowadays most Chinese minority nationalities have already given up the practice. In the Drung River Valley, however, I did come across many women who still performed facial tattooing. Various tattoos formed of round or lozenge-shaped marks in

The Drung River Valley abounds in rare and precious crude drugs and medicinal herbs, such as Chinese goldthread (*Coptis chinensis*), fritillary (*Fritillaria thunbereii*), elevated gastrodia (*Gastrodia elata*), musk and bear's gallbladder.

A Drung village. In most cases, Drung people living in the same village belong to the same clan. A village generally contains only a few families.

greenish blue were seen between their eyebrows, on their cheeks or around their mouths. The pattern of their facial tattoo varies with the clan to which the wearer of facial tattoo belongs, I was told one may identify the stockaded village a Drung woman belongs to by her facial tattoo.

The Drung convention—a very ancient convention indeed!—Dictates that a male infant has to be given a name on the seventh day after his birth, and that a female infant on the ninth day after her birth. The Drung people do not adopt surnames. A Drung name generally consists of: (1) the name of the clan (which is also the name of the place the clan lives in), (2) the name of the infant's father or mother, (3) the infant's pet name, and (4) the infant's position of seniority with regard to its siblings. Take the name of a Drung male, Konggan Pengsong Akeqia Ding, for example; in it "Konggan" is derived from the name of his clan; "Pengsong" is the name of his father; "Akeqia" is his pet name; "Ding" (in Drung patois "Ding" means the fourth) is his position of seniority with regard to his siblings. And he may be addressed in brief simply as "Konggan Ding". Many of the Drung youths I formed acquaintances with have adopted a Sinitic name in addition to a Drung name. The additional Sinitic name is a full name similar to that of a Han people; that is, it is complete with a surname and a name. The surname in an additional Sinitic name of a Drung youth comes from the first syllable in the name of the village he belongs to. For example, the youths from "Maku" village will have the surname of "Ma" in their additional Sinitic names. The youths from "Qidang" village will have the surname of "Qi" in their additional Sinitic names, and the youths from "Kongmu" village will have the surname of "Kong" in their additional Sinitic names.

Life of the Drung People

The Drung River Valley is blessed with a genial climate and favourable rainfall. On the east bank of the Drung River Gaoligong Mountain towers grandly with its summit of more than 5,000 metres above sea level. On the west bank of the river Dandanglika Mountain poses magnificently. When November comes, the tops of the mountains are gradually covered with thick layers of snow, completely obstructing the passages back and forth across these mountains. This renders the Drung River Valley absolutely inaccessible from any direction. It is not until the thaw begins in July or August that the ties between the Drung River Valley and the outside world are reestablished. In the warm season when the mountain passages are open to traffic, the Drung people cross the mountains, thread their ways through the forests, and wade across the swamps, taking with them such local products as medicinal herbs and pelts to barter for necessities such as salt. The social and economic development in the Drung community has been slow and much retarded on account of its being nearly inaccessible geographically. In the early 1950s, only a very few Drung families could afford to buy an ox, and farming in the Drung area was basically in the primitive slash-and-burn cultivation stage. The piece of land which was worked according to the slash-and-burn method was locally called "burned field in the mountain"; on such a tract of land they used to grow maize, bitter buckwheat, highland barley and other similar crops. Now in the plots around their houses they cultivate various species of melons, beans or peas, and other vegetables. They husk their grains by means of wooden mortar and pestle or by stone mill. They do not know how to make use of farm cattle. Though they raised a species called Drung ox, which is very big and heavy, they feed it only for sacrificial purpose. The output of their primitive farming is not sufficient to support their livelihood all the year round, so hunting, fishing, and gathering products of mountain growth have become an indispensable supplementary means for securing their livelihood.

The Drung people have their own way of fishing. They attach a net woven of fine flaxen strings to two long bamboo poles and sink the poles and the net in a river. The fisherman simply sits on the bank and waits for the fish to get entangled in the net.

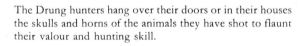

The Drung hunters hang over their doors or in their houses the skulls and horns of the animals they have shot to flaunt their valour and hunting skill.

The crossbow, made of hard wood such as that of a mulberry tree, is the principal hunting weapon of a Drung hunter. A Drung hunter is shown holding a crossbow. The pouch dangling by his side is a container for arrows of various sizes.

There is a popular saying among the Drung folks: "Nobody shall die of starvation here," because there are edible wild plants everywhere in the valley, such as mushroom, wild sweet potato, wild lily and others. The most well-known edible wild plant here is a kind of tree called *alei*. There is rich starch contained in the tissue of the trunk of an alei tree. An experienced old man just bores a little hole into the soil near the root of an alei tree and puts one of his ear to the hole to listen, and then he is able to predict how much starch is contained in the tree. To extract starch from the tree, people fell it, split its trunk, and pulverize the splinters of the split trunk. Then they put the wood powder thus obtained into a bamboo basket and leach out the starch with water. Local people use such starch to cook gruel or *baba* (pastry); it tastes a little sweet.

The Drung women often weave Drung carpet in their upstairs chambers or in the shade of trees. The carpet is made of flax and is one of the distinctive ornaments of this nationality. In the past the Drung people used to twist the fibres of the wild flax into strings and weave them into flaxen cloth—or rather into a carpet. They did not know how to sew then; so both men and women of the Drung nationality has to wrap their bodies with a piece of woven cloth or carpet. Such a carpet served for their dress in the daytime and for their bedding at night. Nowadays, though the Drung people have clothes to put on, still they are in the habit of draping a Drung carpet over their dress. Wearing a Drung carpet, the Drung males customarily leave their left shoulder bare, and the Drung females customarily leave their right shoulder bare. The Drung women like to hang a few strands of beads as ornaments about their necks. Some old people and children wear a string of animals' teeth or bones around their necks, in addition to beads, as ornaments and talismans.

The materials the Drung people use to build their houses include timber, rattan, and bamboo. It is very hot in the lower reaches of the Drung River, where most houses are built of bamboo; such a bamboo structure is always one or two metres above the ground with its back against a hill. The walls and floors of such houses are all made of plaited bamboo strips.

There is a door on either side of the house, and the doors face each other squarely. A suspended corridor is attached to the side which confronts the hill. To a pillar supporting the corridor a wooden pestle with mortar is fixed with ropes. In the Drung River Valley there is a very interesting type of dwelling-house called a "long house." Externally it looks like a building containing only a single room extended to a considerable length. Actually it is composed of several chambers joined together. It houses a large family with its members belonging to different generations assigned to live in different chambers. It is a convention of the Drung people that all the male members of a family should live under the same roof even after they have married. When a male member of the family is going to get married, the family will build for him a new chamber which abuts closely on the long house of the family. Therefore, as the family increases, the long house grows even longer. There is a communication passage in the house, so that all the chambers are mutually accessible within the house. But recently more and more young people give up living in the familial community after they have married; this has almost become a common practice of the Drung younger generation now. And the institution of the communal long house is diminishing.

In the upper reaches of the Drung River, big, thick pieces of sawed planks are used for constructing two-storey dwelling-houses. In such a house, there are one or two shelves made of plaited bamboo strips suspended above the fireplace for depositing cooking utensils or things that need drying. The Drung folk do not furnish their houses with chests or trunks. In a Drung house a board is usually fixed along the wall on which to place miscellaneous things. A hunting knife and a crossbow are inserted into the cracks of the aforesaid board and clothes are hung from a string overhead. They like to hang the skulls of the animals they have hunted from the roof beams of their houses to show their valour and wealth. In a house in Maku village in the lower reaches of the Drung River, I saw more than 20 monkey skulls dangling from the roof beam, besides the skulls of boar, bear, and wild mule.

The granary of a Drung family is always built several metres away from the dwelling place. The granary is supported off the ground on pillars to guard against rats.

Formerly the Drung people wrenched their livelihood from slash-and-burn cultivation, but now they have mastered all the technique of cultivating paddy crops.

Since the dwelling-houses of the Drung people are built with wood and bamboo, they catch fire easily. Their granaries are generally built some distance away from their dwelling-houses and rise directly from the ground. Logs are the principal material for constructing granaries and are fitted into place so closely in the structure that mice can never burrow through them.

The average width of the Drung River is nearly 30 metres. But the drops of the rapids in the river are considerable, which make it a torrent too swift to be navigable. Many bridges made of plaited rattan strips span the Drung River; they have been built by the Drung people. Such bridges have no piers. The body of such a bridge is made of bamboo poles or wood planks fixed together with ropes. And the bridge body is suspended above the water with cables made of twisted strands of rattan. To guard the travellers against tumbling into the water, rattan meshes are stretched underneath the bridge body.

After I had entered the Drung River Valley the first stunt I had to learn to master was to walk over a rattan bridge with a span of about 100 metres. The bridge body, which is a framework of bamboo, is both narrow and slippery — too narrow for my feet to be put down closely side by side. Though the suspension of the bridge has now been changed into steel cables instead of rattan cables, the two iron wires are no more than one metre apart. The moment I trod on the bridge, it began to quiver. The farther I proceeded almost half way, the more terribly it swung. Looking down at the madly racing stream below, I felt as if I had been swept upstream together with the bridge in midair. I grasped the cables desperately to calm down myself; and it was not until some moments later that I could composedly struggle to reach the opposite bank. But a Drung man can walk over the rattan bridge even with a fully loaded basket on his back and proceed as steadily as on a boulevard. The Drung people also dare to cross a rattan bridge in a pitch-dark night. Another means of transit over the Drung River is a bamboo "slide" cable, which is made by twisting strands of bamboo strips together. To cross the river, the courageous Drung men just

The pestles and mortar are worked by two persons. Each of them takes a pestle, and the pestles strike alternately the grain in the hollow of the mortar. The Drung people handle such instruments very deftly in close co-operation.

Wooden pestles and mortar worked manually are instruments very popular with the people living in the Drung River Valley for processing unhusked grain and other food.

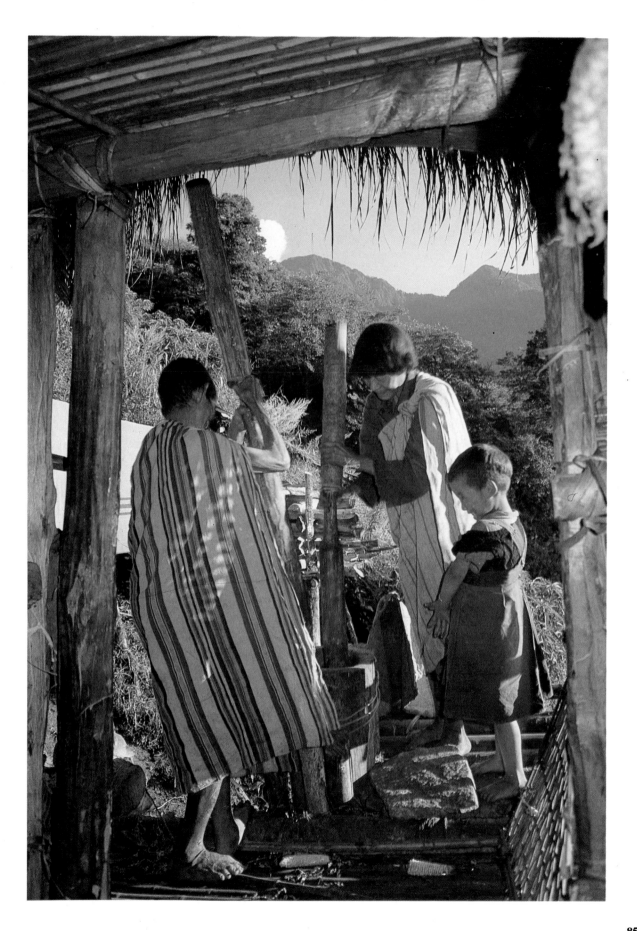

cling to the cable with their hands and feet and crawl quickly hand over hand along the cable. They are completely undisturbed by the roaring and rushing river waters below, when they are on the cable. A very stunning sight indeed for a spectator who comes for the first time from the outside world!

The Rites of Offering Bovine Sacrifice to Heaven

The songs and dances of the Drung people mirror the simple and natural traits of their nationality. Celebrations and harvest seasons are occasions for singing and dancing. On such occasions they will heat a big pot of Drung wine (made of rice) and get together to dance "*Drungpuer*" (the name of a dance) and sing some very ancient arias. These Drung arias tell the real stories of some Drung historic characters and reflect the yearnings on the part of the Drung people for a happy and bright future.

The Drung people keep only one festival, the Spring Festival. It falls on an unfixed date in the eleventh or twelfth lunar month. On this day they observe the rites of offering bovine sacrifice to heaven, and the rites are accompanied by a dance. I chanced to be an eyewitness of this spectacular event at Kongmu Village in the upper reaches of the Drung River.

All the villagers must turn up at the rites. This time the bovine sacrifice was a black bull of seven or eight years old. It might weigh somewhere between 200 or 250 kilogrammes. It looked unrestrainedly fierce and savage with its curved horns pointing maliciously outwards. Somebody went forth to drape it with a Drung carpet and hung several strings of beads about its ears. Being thus trimmed it was led to go around the house of its owner six times, and at the same time the villagers cast the seeds of barnyard grass over its body. After this, it was tethered to a post. Now the people began to drink from the wine pot and dance. Some men, all in their adulthood, began to beat the gongs with sticks whittled from pieces of tree root, and the people moved and danced to the slow tempo of the gongs. They turned their stretched hands in the air and held out their arms towards the sky, as if they were praying for heaven's blessings. The dance was impressive for its charms tinged with mystery and solemnness.

The Drung nationality refrains from using a knife to butcher a bovine sacrifice. They use an instrument called "stunning rod," which is a kind of poisonous bamboo. Two old men with glistening white hair assumed the main role of sacrificing the bull to Heaven. They were draped with Drung carpets, a cup of wine in one hand and a long bamboo headed by the stunning rod in the other. There they stood, looking imposing and militant. They drank ceremonially before they walked away to take up their positions on both sides of the bull. Then they lifted their instruments to pierce the chest of the bull violently. After the animal had fallen to the ground and breathed its last, one of the people cut a lobe off the bull's ear and impaled it upon a twig. Then he whisked the twig to and fro over the bull's carcass and at the same time read prayers. Having finished this ritual he flung the twig as far away as he could. Now they began to dismember the bull. Its head went to the owner of the bull. Both of the bull killers got a big portion of beef off the wound the stunning rod had inflicted. The rest of the villagers were presented with one piece of beef per head. After all the bull's carcass was given away, one of the bull killers carried the bull's head on his back, and the villagers moved in a circle around him and danced. Gradually they worked themselves up to such a frenzy that everybody began to propose "one-cup toasts" to anybody else indiscriminately. Scores of kilogrammes of wine were thus gone in a little while. The two old bull killers got so drunk that they could hardly stand on their own feet; yet they refused to go home to have a nap. Some of the villagers told me that in the past such a dancing carousal would go on for several days.

In the past, gathering mountain products was one of the important sources of income for the Drung people. Nowadays, they still take great pleasure in gathering mountain products, such as the fruits of some wild plants, for no other purpose than varying their diet.

The altitude of the upper reaches of the Drung River is higher than that of its lower reaches. The climate of the upper reaches is rather cold; the staple products of this area are potatoes, buckwheat, corn, and beans. Shown here is a Drung woman in reaping soybeans.

This Drung woman is coiling the coloured hempen threads into balls. A Drung carpet is woven of such threads.

A Drung man always has a Drung carpet draped over him and a chopper by his side. His legs are wrapped in white leggings. The Drung men shown here look militantly smart.

The bright-coloured Drung carpet is an indispensable ornamental part of the dress of the Drung people. To manufacture it, the Drung women first spin hemp fibre into threads and dye the threads red, yellow, blue, green, or violet. Then they use a simple loom to weave the threads of various colours into a striped carpet.

When a male member of a Drung family is going to get married, a new chamber is constructed for him at one end of the house the family lives in. The new chamber must be so closely connected with the house that the two look like a single building, not like two separated buildings standing together. With the continual additions of new chambers, the house is gradually elongated into a long single row.

A few bamboo poles are bound together suspended from two steel or rattan cables spanning a channel; such a structure serves to bridge over the Drung River and is called a rattan bridge.

The Drung River rolls violently under the rattan bridge. Standing at the middle of the bridge and gazing dizzily into the madly racing current in the river, one can scarcely tell whether the turbulent water below or the rattan bridge is really on the move. Therefore the local folk nickname the rattan bridge "a bridge ever on the move."

On the Threshold of Modern Life

The Drung nationality is rather underdeveloped culturally and economically compared with the people living in the developed areas in China. Some aspects of the life in the Drung populated areas may even be regarded as somewhat primitive. However, the Drung nationality is not destined to be forsaken by history. For some decades modern civilization has been gradually permeating the Drung River Valley.

Improvement in transport facilities is critical to bringing about a marked improvement in the material life of the Drung people. In the 1960s the local administration constructed a passage for caravans from Kongshan County through the Drung River Valley. Later, several main passages in the valley were constructed; two suspension cable bridges open to caravan traffic were completed, and 13 minor cable bridges were built. Three small-scale hydropower stations have also been constructed in the valley. In the warm season when the passages in the mountains surrounding the Drung River Valley are passable, the local administration dispatch-es caravans to deliver large quantities of salt, piece goods, tobacco, tea and other necessities and means of production to the Drung people in the valley.

In the past, the Drung people did not know how to raise pigs and they kept oxen not for ploughing their land but for sacrificial purposes. The People's Liberation Army frontier guards stationed in the valley took it upon themselves to initiate the Drung people into the husbandry of pigs and inland oxen and into the use of oxen for farming. Pigsties or cattle sheds are seen everywhere in the villages nowadays. The local administration has also made efforts to popularize the technique of

The animal chosen as the sacrificial ox to Heaven, is draped with a Drung carpet and decorated with strings of coloured beads about its ears. Then it is led to walk around the house of its owner six times before the ceremony.

These Drung people are dancing slowly to the tempo of a deliberately sounding ritual gong. This marks the beginning of the bovine sacrifice.

Charged with the sacred duty of killing the sacrificial ox are two old men highly respected by the villagers. They drink a "one-cup toast" to each other before they start to dance with their stunning rods.

After the ox is dead, the Drung people flay it, and every family in the village is presented a portion of its beef. Throughout the ritual of bovine sacrifice, the dance goes on unchecked and will often continue for a couple of days after the sacrificial rite.

The killers of the sacrificial ox pierce its heart with the sharpened stunning rods.

The local county administration organizes caravans for transporting into the Drung River Valley the means of production and daily necessities. The caravans have to cross mountains, penetrate forests and struggle along for many days before they reach their destinations.

With the advent of the warm season and after the accumulated snow that has blocked the mountain passages to the Drung River Valley has thawed, caravans come to the stockaded villages of the Drung people.

The caravans are the purveyors of daily necessities for the Drung people. Even the people from the Qiu nationality that live beyond the border but speak the Drung patois cross the border and go to the supply-and-marketing cooperative in a Drung village to barter their crude drugs, medicinal herbs, and pelts for daily necessities.

paddy cultivation in the valley. Now the Drung people have rice to add to their diet. Schools, hospitals, shops, and post and telecommunications offices have been established in the Drung River area. I was able to make a trunk call to Beijing from there. The administration of the Gongshan Drung-Nu Autonomous County was founded in 1956. The county head, Kong Zhiqing, is a Drung man. The population of the Drung people was just over 1,700 in the early 1950s, but grew to over 4,000 by 1982.

I chanced to pass a National Day (October 1) during my journalistic tour through the Drung River Valley. There was something unique about the liveliness and vigour in the holiday celebration held in this remote valley. Though there was no gala decoration, fanfare or feast here, the ebullient mirth shown by the local people on such an occasion was like that displayed by their counterpart in Beijing or Shanghai. Man and woman basketball matches between teams from different villages contested with vigour. The man and woman

players, hailing from distant stockaded villages and looking smart in their red sportswear with the collars of their shirts flaring about their necks, came to play but I did not expect they could play so well! Come to think of it, what a change! Their parents not only had not been privileged so much as to touch a basketball but even could hardly have proper clothes to cover their bodies in their youth. On that night when a bonfire was raised on the basketball playground, hundreds of people were instantly attracted. Now the people joined hands to form a huge circle around the bonfire and danced. At first they performed a Tibetan dance. Soon some people detached themselves from the crowd and formed a circle of their own. Then a pipe trilled in the midst of the people forming the new circle, which began to perform a dance of the Lisu nationality.

The Drung River Valley is adjacent to the areas inhabited by both the Tibetan and Lisu nationalities. So the Drung people in the valley are culturally very much influenced by their neighbouring nationalities. All of a sudden,

The picturesque banks of the Drung River are always the scenes of intimate *tête-à-tête* between lovers.

music from a tape recorder was heard playing *"Strolling Along a Village Path."* I was curious to know how modern contrivance like cassette tape recorders had come to settle in such a culturally out-of-the-way place as this. Tracing the source of the music, I found several cassette tape recorders playing there. A group of youth gathered around these recorders of various brands were dancing to the music. The recorders played and played, and the throng surrounding them became bigger and bigger; eventually even the middle-aged women with little tots on their backs were drawn to the recorders and danced too. Now, on the playground, there was a merry hullabaloo of tape-recorder music, singing and piping. Kerosene was poured over the bonfire to make it burn more furiously. The glow from the bonfire crimsoned the heartily laughing faces of these Drung people. The scene was very touching for me indeed. These people, who, according to historians, struggled to survive by "seeking shelter in rocky caves in the mountains," "clothing themselves in foliage," and "eating birds and animals raw" before the last one or two centuries and were called "primitive human beings," have now skipped long historical stages and are making great strides towards modern life.

The youth are the liveliest part of village population. They gather in the evenings to enjoy themselves dancing and singing late into the night.

The Nu People
on the Banks of the Nu
River

The riverbed of the Nu River is a great depression; the vertical elevations between the riverbed and the tops of the ridges forming the banks of the river range between 3,000 and 4,000 metres. The canyon of the Nu River is one of the most famous canyons in the world. Actually the banks of the Nu River are formed of precipices, and Nu people have bored a passage for themselves on the ledges across the middle of the precipices.

The Nu River rises in the Tanggula Mountains in the Tibet Autonomous Region. It flows southwards for hundreds of kilometres in China.

The Nu River rages between Biluo Mountain and Gaoligong Mountain, these two mountains being parts of the Hengduan Mountain Range. The river rolls south into Burma and is called the Salween River by the Burmese; finally it empties into the Indian Ocean. Shown here is the landscape of the upper reaches of the Nu River; the course of the river describes a huge semi-circle enclosing the foot of Biluo Mountain. On the slope of the mountain is situated a stockaded village of the Nu nationality.

Did the Nu River borrow its name from the Nu nationality? Or the other way round? So far nobody can provide an authentic answer to these questions. But in a Tang Dynasty official publication entitled *A Book on the Life of Aborigines in the South Frontier* written more than 10 centuries ago, there is a record concerning the Nu River. In the Nu nationality's language the Nu River is called "Numigua"; "Nu" means swarthy in that language, and "migua" means river water.

The total population of this nationality amounts to over 23,000; most of them live in the three counties of Gongshan, Fugong, and Bijiang in Yunnan Province, with the Nu River flowing past all three counties. A small portion of the Nu nationality is distributed in the two counties of Weixi and Lanping. Those Nu people who inhabit the upper reaches of the Nu River call themselves "Nu" or "Anu." Those

Nu people who populate the lower reaches of the Nu River choose to call themselves "Nusu." The linguistic difference between the two branches — the upper reaches branch and the lower reaches branch — of the Nu nationality is so great that they cannot communicate without an interpreter. And they differ immensely in traditions and customs. These facts give rise to the inference that in its earlier development the Nu nationality assimilated several national elements. Diverse ancient tribes or hordes had migrated to the Nu River area and settled down there; they gradually merged finally into a single national community with each of them still clinging to the special characteristics of its own.

My coverage concerns the life in the Bingzhongluo Nu-inhabited area in the county of Gongshan, a county in the upper reaches of the Nu River.

A Harvest Season in the Bingzhongluo Area

A highway stretches in the direction of the upper reaches of the Nu River; it now winds at the foot of Biluo Mountain — with its top perennially snow-clad — to the east of the river; it then runs before Gaoligong Mountain to the west of the river. The two mountains run from north to south in parallel and relentlessly sandwich the violent and recalcitrant Nu River between them. The vertical elevations of the mountain peaks along the banks of the river range from 3,000 to 4,000 metres. It is a marvelous grand canyon-like landscape. The river roars and rushes at the speed of three or four metres per second. I was rather tempted to think the river was straining to tear away from the restraint the two mountains imposed upon it. Spanning the river are not only ancient cable bridges but also modern suspension cable bridges. This odd juxtaposition of the old and the new civilization may be symbolic of the cultural transition the nationalities living in the Nu River region are now experiencing.

Bingzhongluo area can be reached by travelling on foot northwards from Gongshan County in two days. Two flat "toes" of Biluo Mountain protrude unexpectedly from under its precipice at some distance to the south of the Bingzhongluo area. Here the Nu River has to bypass the "toes" and thus describes a big semi-circle looking roughly like a U. The stream flowing in this U-shaped bend is rather placid. I saw some Nu people fishing in the bend in their canoes. A beautiful tableland stands to the north of the river bend. Further north looms the perennially snow-covered peak of Gaoligong Mountain. The slope of the

Bingzhongluo, a tableland, is an expanse of elevated flatland in a mountain in the upper reaches of the Nu River. It is one of the most populous areas inhabited by the Nu nationality.

The loud tamping of pestles against mortars is heard everywhere in the harvest season in a Nu village.

As soon as the harvest season is over, the Nu people have to plunge into tilling their land. The plough they use is drawn by two draft oxen, and such a way of yoking is known as "two-oxen-carry-a-bar."

The Nu people do their sowing by first scattering seeds on the soil and then by turning the soil over with a plough.

During busy seasons, villagers help each other with farm work. A household has to prepare beforehand enough wine and delicacies for the neighbours who come to help with sowing or reaping.

mountain is a bizarre mosaic of variform paddy fields in which the people have recently harvested their paddy crops. Interspersed among the paddy fields are houses with glistening white walls and roof-tops covered with stone slabs. The area these houses are in is called Bingzhongluo which has over 50 villages under its care and is populated by more than 8,000 people. The majority of the population are the Nu people, who have all along managed to preserve their own customs and way of living. They keep to themselves and lead a calm and simple life.

The wife of a villager whose neighbours have come to help with farm work is seen in the field serving the helpers with sweet *gudu* wine.

The agriculture of the Nu nationality is more advanced than that of the Drung people; the system of private ownership of arable land is basically regulated in the Nu community. The Nu people lay great emphasis on fertilizing their land. An average household in a Nu village can raise as many as three or four oxen as draft animals. The Nu people generally yoke two oxen to a plough, which is rigged up to a thick wooden bar; the traces of the two farm cattle are fixed to both ends of the wooden bar. So the local people call this way of yoking "two-oxen-carry-a-bar." The staple products here include wheat, corn, buckwheat, and highland barley. Some parts of Bingzhongluo, which have a mild climate, grow paddy crops.

By mid-November, the Nu people in the Nu River Valley are involved in their busiest season of a year which is devoted to working on autumn harvest and sowing. The villagers are zealously developing co-operation in farm work. In the busiest season, a villager may ask any other villager to help with his reaping and sowing. The helpers are entertained to handsome dinner but never ask for any other reward. Jia Mucheng, in whose house I took up my temporary lodging when I was touring the Nu people's area, asked six villagers to sow the seeds of highland barley for him in his plot. To sow the seeds over the soil of a plot of land is the first and primary step in the whole process of sowing; a good harvest presupposes a dexterous and timely sowing of the seeds.

Therefore, the Nu people are all very careful in timing the operation of seed-sowing.

Early in the morning of the day set for seed-sowing, Jia Mucheng laid a table laden with offerings in front of the fireplace. The things Jia piously set forth on the table include the grains of five cereal plants, a bunch of flowers, a bunch of pine needles, and a lamp fueled with butter. He kindled the lamp as soon as he had laid the table. To entertain the six helpers, he prepared buttered tea, mild wine, roasted *baba,* stewed taro, and other food. It is the convention of the Nu people that a pig or pigs must be killed on the day of seed-sowing. But the pig to be sacrificed on that day should be a suckling weighing no more than 10 kilogrammes. Great fat hogs are preserved for the entertainment in the Spring Festival. The helpers ate breakfast at their own homes, shouldered the ploughs and led their oxen to Jia's home and from there Jia and his helpers set out to his field. They sowed the highland barley seeds over the soil and turned up the soil with ploughs drawn by oxen. Though these helpers came to join the job for friendship sake they worked most strenuously. Their sonorous commands to the oxen mingling with their light-hearted laughing and talking rang merrily over Jia's field.

In the gathering dusk, they came back to Jia's home and had a dinner together around the fireplace. The dinner was sumptuous, and they ate it in a most cordial atmosphere as if they were really of one family. *Gudu* wine (a mild alcoholic drink brewed of corn) and *gudufan* (cooked corn grain, which is unhusked and finely pestled) are two favourites indispensable to such feasts. Jia put the sweet and sticky *gudufan* in a bamboo crate. The guests would help themselves to the gudufan. They used chopsticks — measuring about 40 centimetres long — to dig up a lump of

With a day's labour over, all the helpers are invited to the dinner party at the house of the land owner. A reward the owner of the land offers to his helpers, the dinner also serves as an occasion for a happy get-together after having worked shoulder to shoulder in the field.

gudufan from the crate. Then committing the lump of gudufan to his left hand, he nibbled at it, while with his right hand wielding the chopsticks he plied himself with titbits from the dishes on the table. To show his gratitude to his helpers Jia served them delicacies like stewed pig's trotters and taro, stewed sucklings, soup of bean curd and pig blood, crisp and sweet roasted baba. Baba is generally made of buckwheat flour. There are two species of buckwheat: the sweet buckwheat and the bitter buckwheat. The Nu people do not use a frying-pan for roasting baba. Instead, they use a kind of frying slab they quarry in the depth of a mountain. They first heat the slab on a tripod over the fireplace; then they spread the watery dough of buckwheat flour over the heated slab. When one side of the spread dough is done, the dough is turned over for roasting the other side. A multi-layer baba can be roasted by spreading more than one layer of dough one after another. This kind of slab has

the property of transmitting heat evenly to all its parts, and it never cracks under the action of heat. It is counted as one of the indispensable cooking facilities of the Nu people.

Though I did not go to help with seed-sowing in Jia's field, still as a guest coming from afar. I was invited to the dinner Jia gave in honour of his six helpers Thus I was given the pleasure of enjoying the mirth bred of their *esprit de corps*. The host, warmhearted and hospitable, while earnestly helping his guests to all the dishes, sang laudatory songs to express his thanks to all the helpers as well as his delight in having me as a lodger in his house. The host and his guests became more excited after the first round of toasts; people began to sing while helping each other to the dishes and became more at home and intimate as if they were all of one family. After the dinner they began to dance, circling about the central pillar in the chamber until late into the night when their mothers or wives came to

A family busily thrashing buckwheat they have just reaped.

After the harvest season, the Nu women go back to their looms again to weave blankets.

After the harvest season, the Nu men prepare their equipment before going to hunt in the mountains.

Jia's to summon them home. The institution of cooperation in farm work can be traced far back to the primitive practice of mutual assistance. This practice had been followed generation after generation and has evolved into the present social behaviour of cooperation in farm work. It is a manifestation of the traditional virtue common to the Nu people.

Dimuwa — A Solemn Marriage Ceremony

I had been told long ago that the Nu nationality has an interesting custom referred to as *dimuwa*. In the Nu patois, dimuwa means a solemn marital rite. But dimuwa is not conducted on the occasion of the wedding of a young couple, but on the occasion of certain anniversary — that is, on the twentieth, thirtieth, fortieth, fiftieth, or sixtieth anniversary — of a long-married couple. Not all the old married couples are eligible for holding dimuwa; only those that live a really harmonious married life and have never been visited by quarrel or fighting with the fisticulffs between man and wife are qualified for holding the grand ceremony of dimuwa. I discovered a married couple living in the village of Jiasheng and preparing to observe ceremonious dimuwa. The husband is called Xilong, and the wife Nanzhen. They have married for 20 years. They had originally planned to observe their dimuwa during the Spring Festival. The villagers suggested that the dimuwa to be held in their honour be advanced, so that I, a visitor from a faraway land, could offer them, the blissful couple, my best wishes at their dimuwa. Besides, their reaping of corn and buckwheat was already finished. So, the date of their dimuwa was thus advanced.

The roof beam of this couple's house was draped with many layers of cobs of corn. Many jars of gudu wine were brought into the house. (Their house is built of logs.) A table was laid, on which was spread a layer of green pine needles. The green pine leaves symbolize the connubial fidelity and concord of this married couple. The four corners of the table were sprinkled with buckwheat flour, which is a token of bountifulness and prosperity. On the day set for observing their first dimuwa, Xilong and Nanzhen would become a "bridegroom" and "bride" again. She put on a silver breast-ornament which she had worn on her wedding day 20 years ago. The relatives, friends and neighbours of this couple who came to attend the dimuwa were all in their gala dress. On the right-hand side of the fireplace sitting in a row were Xilong's parents, relatives and friends. On the left-hand side of the fireplace were Nanzhen's parents, relatives and friends. On the altar, which was at the front of and a little higher than the fireplace, were lit two lamps; grains of corn and thin wine were also laid on the altar, which was decorated with needle-shaped pine leaves. After all the guests had arrived, the dimuwa commenced. The "bride," the "bridegroom," and their two children entered the hall where the fireplace was and where the dimuwa was to be held. Their boy was a teenager who came in before the parents, and their daughter was still a toddler, carried on her mother's back. The "bridegroom" and his "bride" together held a wooden platter in their hands; the platter was covered with pine leaves on which sat pieces of buckwheat baba. They politely offered these to all their elders. Then the "bridegroom" took off his cap, and the "bride" removed her scarf before they knelt down and kowtowed reverently to the shrine of their ancestors on the altar over the fireplace. After that they kowtowed to all their elders. Having

Nanzhen now puts on her ornament which she pinned on her coat on her wedding day 20 years ago; she is going to be a "bride" again.

Nanzhen and her husband Xilong are going to be a "bride" and a "bridegroom" again; they will go over their "marriage ceremony" as before. Also shown are their two children.

Nanzhen, the bride, and Xilong, the bridegroom, are proposing toasts to their elders attending their *dimuwa*.

The elders give gifts to the bride and the bridegroom and express the hope that the "new couple" will lead a happier and more harmonious life.

The bride and the bridegroom offer sweets to the villagers who come to congratulate them.

completed these rites, the "bride" took hold of a thick and large bamboo tube filled with wine, and the "bridegroom" held a cup in his hands. Then they proposed a toast to each of their elders in turn. They also proposed toasts to all their relatives and friends. After the toasts, the elders gave their presents to the "bride" and the "bridegroom." The "bridegroom" was presented with a silver-inlaid wooden bowl, and the "bride" a pair of silver bracelets. Two old grannies put the silver bracelets on the "bride's" arms. All those who were present gave the "bride" and the "bridegroom" the blessings that their married life was going to be happier and more harmonious, and that their dimuwa might be celebrated again and again in future anniversaries of their marriage.

Then the "bride" and the "bridegroom" together with the guests raised their cups and drank toasts and began to sing a popular song of the Nu people to express their best wishes for the couple. The "bride" and the "bridegroom" started to dance; the rest in the hall followed suit. They moved around the central pillar of the hall dancing and singing. The hall, with a floor space of scores of square metres, now accommodated as many as 100 people. At the end of a song they would shout, "Go on dancing, please!" And the log building shook again with the heavy stampings of the dancers. All the wine in the "bridegroom's" house was exhausted, but many of the guests went away and returned soon with jars of wine fetched from their homes. They went on dancing in Xilong's house, though it was towards the small hours. When some of them were too tired to dance, they would just crouch beside the fireplace and take a nap. Awaked from their doze, they would raise their bamboo cups again and rejoin the dancing party. The little baby carried on the "bride's" back had been asleep for quite some time, and on its sweet and tender face still lingered the trace of a gratified smile. For sure, it was sharing the bliss of dimuwa held in her parents' honour. Of

The celebration of the marriage ceremony reaches its climax when the "new couple" and the guests rise to dance.

This small stockaded village, called Chugan, hidden deep in a valley is a Nu village in the north of Yunnan and on the common border of Yunnan and Tibet.

course, the "bridegroom" Xilong and his "bride" Nanzhen were the most mirthful and happiest of all those who were present; they had been devoted to and most affectionate towards each other consistently for two decades, and they had won the respect of the whole village. It seems quite safe to predict that their married life is bound to continue to be satisfactory in the future.

Qingnatong — A Village in the North of Yunnan

Having bid adieu to Jiasheng Village, I continued my tour, proceeding northwards along the Nu River, and I came to a stockaded village called Qingnatong. Actually it is an "administrative" village, which is composed of four "geographical" villages. One of the villages called Chugan is at the extreme north of Yunnan and populated mostly by the Nu people. If you set out from Chugan, cross a perennially snow-capped mountain, and walk for a solid day, you are bound to be in the Chawalong region in Tibet.

Qingnatong is a place noted for its abundant production of walnuts. The Nu people here build their houses in the shade of the walnut trees their forefathers had planted. The roofs of the houses of the Nu people are usually covered with stone slabs for tiles; the architecture of their buildings is uniform. They are neat and quaint in their own way. The cliffs and rocks in the mountain here are also unusual. They are formed of vertical, rather than horizontal, strata, and the strata look like books placed vertically together on a shelf. A big chunk of such stone can readily be carved off a cliff and can be easily ripped asunder. The thinness of such a stratum may be less than half a centimetre. All the strata of such a chunk of stone will be cut into different sizes and shapes to suit the needs of roofing. These stone slabs, when used for tiles, are laid on the rooftop in a herringbone pattern. Such a stone slab does not crack or break even if a hole is bored into it or a nail is driven through it.

I was told that formerly some French missionaries had come to the Nu River Valley and built their churches with such stone slabs. The space between the roof and the ceiling of a Nu people's house is used for storing the unprocessed food grains of the latest harvest. A house here generally contains several rooms; the parents and their children live in separate rooms. There is a guest-room in the house exclusively for receiving visitors. There is a fireplace in the guest-room, around which the family members eat their meals at ordinary times. Under the floor of the house is an excavation about one metre in depth. The excavation is used as a pigsty or cattle shed.

When a hoe or some farm tool is seen hitched to the door of a house, it means all the household has gone to a distant place to do farm work. If the door of a house is only roughly fastened on the outside, it means that the owner of the house is certainly not far off.

Before my visit to Chugan, it was virtually an unknown land to all outsiders. So I got an unusually warm reception there. The villagers, who had been strangers to me before, became my close acquaintances in the few days I stayed with them. Each day of my sojourn in the village, the villagers came to my lodgings to give me eggs and food as gifts and fervently asked me to visit them at their homes. Each evening during my stay in their village my place was overcrowded with the villagers. We sat around the fireplace, singing, dancing, and playing bamboo mouth organs, and talking about the legends and folk-tales of the Nu people. Though few of these villagers knew my tongue, and could only communicate with me through an interpreter, still our intimacy grew and grew despite the linguistic impediments. Honest and innocent people naturally attract and are held to one another in feeling, it seemed to me.

All the villagers gathered to see me off the day I left Qingnatong. An old couple, who were over 80, took my hands and asked me to stay in the village for a few more days. They were so passionately bent on keeping me that I, normally a very tough guy, was almost moved to tears. Some of the villagers gathered around me, while others earnestly hustled me to their homes. I could not help but drop in at one villager's house for a little chat and at another's for drinking a toast. The whole morning passed in simply enjoying their sincere hospitality. When I finally swung into the saddle and turned back to wave good-bye to them, I noticed that many old men and women were rubbing the tears off their cheeks with the backs of their hands. I feel from the bottom of my heart that though the seclusion of their gullies and ravines has barred these villagers from access to the outside world, yet their isolation contributes to preserving in them the beautiful virtue and sincere feeling peculiar to the unpolluted primitive mankind.

The compartment between the ceiling and the roof of a house is for storing grain; the space here is protected from rain and properly ventilated.

The Nu people often treat their guests to such game as pheasant or river deer. Such small animals are often caught by some simple trapping devices.

A Nu girl cooks the main item of staple food of the Nu nationality, called *gudufan*, which is prepared from the finely pestled corn.

The walls of the Nu people's houses are constructed of planks, with slabs of stone for roofing.

The Lisu People —A Merry Nationality

Fugong County is situated near the Nu River. It is densely inhabited by the Lisu people, a nationality reported to have an ingrained preference for wine and dance.

A Lisu village nestling against the foot of Biluo Mountain.

Laden with the sorrow of parting, I bade farewell to the Gongshan Autonomous County of the Drulg and Nu nationalities and drove southwards along the Nu River; our car seemed racing against the rolling billows in the river. It took me four hours to reach Fugong County, a place densely populated by the Lisu people.

Fugong is a mountainous county and criss-crossed by many streams. To the east of the county is the perennially snow-capped Biluo Mountain; to the west is Gaoligong Mountain. Both mountains are over 4,000 metres above sea level. The Nu River and the Lancang River carve two tremendous longitudinal canyons between these two mountains. The Lisu people consciously call themselves "the masters of the Lancang River, the Nu River, and the Gold Sand River." The ancestors of the Lisu people had settled before the 8th century in the areas adjacent to a river, which is now called the Yalong River in Sichuan Province, and also adjacent to that segment of the Gold Sand River that separates Sichuan Province and Yunnan Province. After the 16th century, repeated and large-scale migrations took this nationality, through gradual penetration, into areas surrounding the Lancang River and the Nu River. This development has resulted in a peculiar population distribution — widely scattered localities of concentrated inhabi-tation. There are over 466,900 Lisu people in China. Over 186,000 of them live in the Nujiang Autonomous Prefecture of the Lisu nationality, while the rest are scattered in less than 20 counties in the two provinces of Yunnan and Sichuan. The tribes of this nationality distinguish themselves by the colour of their dresses. The Lisu people are divided into three tribes: the White Lisu Tribe, the Black Lisu Tribe, and the Variegated Lisu Tribe. Fugong County is inhabited by the Black Lisu Tribe.

Another Lisu village, located on a tableland between a hill and a stream.

In former days communications between the two banks of the Nu River relied heavily on cables spanning the river. A traveller crossed the river by climbing with his hands and feet along the cable or simply holding on to an inclined cable that helped him slide to the opposite bank.

Now many suspension bridges have been built over the Nu River, strong enough to carry trucks.

There is a colossal round hole in one of the rocky peaks of Gaoligong Mountain. The hole looks like a full moon. The Lisu people call it "the petrified moon." A legend says that a divine shepherd, Adeng by name, fell in love with Ala, the daughter of the Dragon King (the legendary reigning god of the sea) of the East Sea. Ignoring the obstruction imposed by the Dragon King to their nuptial union, they came down from heaven to earth. The offended Dragon King tried to flood the earth with billowy surges rushing inland from the sea to drown them and sink them to the bottom of the sea. When the sea water was about to submerge Gaoligong Mountain, Adeng took out his magic bow and shot a magic arrow through one of the rocky peaks of the mountain. The inundating sea water rushed elsewhere through the hole in the rocky peak where the magic arrow had penetrated. Thus Adeng and Ala survived the deluge and were united. That is why there is the colossal round hole in the shape of a full moon in the rocky peak.

Lisu girls come to the riverside to fetch water. They carry the water back home in long bamboo stems.

Lisu women picking tangerines. Tangerines are one of the staple products in many Lisu villages. In deep autumn the tangerine trees around these villages are heavily laden with golden tangerines.

In the Nu River Valley the climate is genial and the vegetable farms of the Lisu people are lush all the year round.

When the crop is ripening, wild animals, including bears, come to the field to ravage it. The Lisu people wait for the animals and kill them with crossbows.

The Lisu people live in bamboo dwellings constructed off the ground and resting on a great many erect bamboo supports or wooden pillars. They are called "numerous-legged buildings." Such structures are dry, secure from intrusion by wild animals, easy to build and not difficult to move to a new location. The upper area is for the household to live in and the space below the floor is for a pigsty or cattle shed. Such a structure has to be renovated once every three years. On the occasion of renovating or building such dwellings, neighbours will come to lend a hand.

The floor and the walls are made of plaited bamboo strips.

In the 1920s, some Western missionaries came to the Nu River Valley to preach their religions and there are still many Christian churches and chapels in this area. Shown here is a Christmas meeting in one of the local churches.

When the church-going women come to the church with their babies in the baskets on their backs, they hang the baskets to the pags on the wall enclosure of the crudely-built, yet solemn-looking church.

At a Lisu Fair

A highway runs through Fugong County. To the east of the highway standing in the distance are the peaks of snow-crested Biluo Mountain; there are row upon row of new multi-storeyed buildings at the foot of the mountain. The undulating waves of the Nu River can be seen raging to the west of the highway. The day I arrived in Fugong County the local people were holding their township fair, which falls on every fifth day. A section of the highway was occupied by the fairground, which stretched for half a kilometre with busy swarms of Lisu people coming expressly for the occasion. My driver tooted his horn energetically to keep our car inching through the crowd.

Though it was early winter, there were still fair stalls selling fresh and tender vegetables, such as pea shoots and pakchois — greens that smelled of the fresh breath of spring. On the shelves in the trading booths built in a row at the wayside were fresh pork, beef, bamboo mouth-organs (a favourite with the Lisu girls), and crossbow, an indispensable item with the Lisu young men. Little piggies or fat hens cooped up in flat bamboo baskets were for sale also. There was a state-owned shop at the fair with all kinds of daily necessities on display. In order to attract to itself a larger clientele, a tape-recorder in the shop was incessantly playing popular songs of the Lisu people.

The busiest hours of the fair occurred from 10 a.m., when the sun peeped from behind the peaks of Biluo Mountain, to 4 p.m., when the sun began to take its shelter behind the crest of Gaoligong Mountain. Around the noon, the whole length of the fairground was jammed almost to a standstill. The Lisu men tended to gather about the cattle market at the

This Lisu woman is seen carrying her baby in the basket on her back and walking her sheep to the fair, where she intends to sell animals.

A Lisu couple driving their pigs to the fair for sale.

roadside and inspect the livestock driven there for sale; now and then they would drop some offhand little comments on some particular animals. The Lisu women drifted in and out of the grocery or clothes stalls hunting for fancy dresses, ornaments, or gewgaws. A Lisu girl will deliberately dress herself up in a black garment and a long white skirt to go to the fair. For her headdress, she would put on an *oulei* cap, which is woven of strings of red and white beads and patches of conch. Necklaces of strung coloured beads glittered on her breast. Strapped aslant across her chest is an ornamental belt, which is made of big, round patches of conch, looking like the sash decoration a marshal might wear.

The fair exemplifies the colourful life of the Lisu people. Take a turn here and many interesting things are bound to meet your eyes. A Lisu adult of either sex habitually dangles a long pipe from his or her mouth. The tube of the pipe is made of a piece of gnarled purple bamboo stem, and the bowl of the pipe is a lump of hollowed tubular root of bamboo, the lump having on its surface the dense, circular and natural veins of bamboo fibres. The pipe is really an exquisite and practical *objet d' art.* What struck me most unusually is that the pipes of some Lisu people are about one metre

long. I gather a smoker with such a pipe must be exerting himself monstrously drawing at it.

A Lisu woman totting a toddler on her back is also a sight to see at the fair. A baby is generally placed in a basket of fine bamboo strips made especially for this purpose. The basket together with its human occupier is secured in position on a woman's back by means of a smooth-plaited rattan belt, which passes across her forehead. From these baskets on their mothers' backs the toddlers of this nationality are privileged to be introduced to the magnificent sights of the lofty snow-capped mountains and the ever frantic Nu River. When they are tired of watching natural or domestic scenes from the rocking perches on their mothers' backs, they may doze off happily in the midst of the rhythmic walking movements of their mothers' feet.

As far as the Lisu people are concerned, to go to the fair is not only for buying or selling something but also for going out on a spree. The occasion also means for them to be hobnobbing. Accordingly wine is in its own right associated with dancing and singing. Every stall selling drinks at the fair was without exception crowded by different groups of fair-goers seeking pleasure from their cups. When the sun was down and the fair

This Lisu woman is called Wang Maduo. She is over 50 now but lively as when she was young, and is very fond of singing, dancing, and sauntering about at the fair as she did when she was young. The local folk say that she "is regularly present at every fair and regularly likes to drink at every fair."

The local people put their domestic animals and poultry in flat bamboo baskets and carry them to the fair for sale.

Trying on newly bought sneakers.

was going to wind up, these drinkers were already more than half inebriated. Whistling away at their bamboo mouth-organs and strumming their *qiebens* (stringed instrument somewhat similar to a banjo), they left the fair dancing and singing until their retreating figures were completely engulfed in the gathering dusk.

The Lisu people enjoy drinking to gross intoxication. Getting quite drunk, for them, is not a disgraceful behaviour but an honourable act. Even in a quarrel, one tends to cow his opponent by contemptuously badgering him to answer the question: "How often have you got drunk at the wine shops in Fugong County?"

The wine made by the breweries of this nationality is called "tamped wine." It is brewed of maize, Chinese sorghum, or seeds of the barnyard grass. Having fermented grains, a Lisu brewer puts them and some water in a cauldron and boils them; during the boiling process he uses a wooden ladle to tamp the grains repeatedly. Having boiled the grains sufficiently, he puts them into a basket woven of very fine bamboo strips for draining the liquid (that is the tamped wine) from the boiled grains. A Lisu host loves to treat his guests to tamped wine and will never let them leave his house in a sober state; otherwise the host may be considered as rather miserly and looked down upon.

Having just secured my lodgings after I arrived in Fugong County, I was invited by He Junyi, a Lisu functionary working with Fugong County Administration, to his evening tamped wine party. Succumbing to the irresistible encouragement of my host, I went through many drinking bouts, draining cup after cup along with those at the party. At last the host proposed a "unison toast" to me; then other guests followed suit by proposing the same toast to me by turns. Proposing a unison toast is the highest tribute paid to a noble guest, according to the Lisu custom. When drinking such a toast, the proposer should put one of his cheeks in physical contact with that of the one to be treated, so that they can drink from the same cup in a unison toast. In the past in pledging faith to an agreement or convention or to sworn brotherhood, the parties concerned proposed a unison toast to each other. When one party proposed a unison toast, the other party should by no means decline to accept it; a refusal to drink a unison toast with its proposer was a glaring insult to him. At that evening party I fell into stupefaction immediately after having drained a dozen cups of unison toast. And I cannot remember at all how they took me back to my lodgings that evening.

At the Wedding of a Lisu Couple

At the time of the year when all the reaping and sowing in the field had been accomplished and the annual work cycle had already come to an end, the people in the Nu River canyon were agog with joyous enthusiasm about winding up the business of the passing year and preparing for celebrating the advent of the new year. And it was regarded as a highly suitable time for the young unmarried people to have their weddings.

I had the honour of being invited to the wedding of a young Lisu couple at a stockaded village called Lazhudi. The day I arrived at the bridegroom's house, his family was busily engaged in killing an ox, sheep, and pig. Big chunks of meat were hung cheek by jowl from the beam of the kitchen. Many large crates of cooked ground grains of corn were left on the floor. The marriage ceremony was scheduled to be conducted in a multi-level bamboo house; this type of bamboo building is called by the local people "a numerous-legged building," because it rests on many wooden piles. Neither new furniture, new bedding, nor other nuptial appurtenances were visible in the bride's chamber, which was as simply furnished as an ordinary living room. The host told me that the Lisu custom is not to accumulate such things as

Villagers going to attend a marriage ceremony with their presents in the baskets on their backs.

furniture, bedding, and household gear but demands that the new couple strive to create everything from scratch.

The next day was set for the wedding. Many a villager had come to lend a helping hand since the early morning. A good number of the youths went into the mountain to cut bamboos and brought them back; then they sawed them up joint by joint. Every joint was to be used at the feast as a cup for drinking wine. The little girls took all the sawed joints to the fountain and washed them clean. A host has to provide as many bamboo cups as there are guests in the house. On this occasion, the host prepared so many bamboo cups that they alone filled up several crates.

Everything in the hall upstairs dedicated to the observance of the marriage ceremony had already been put in neat order. The water in the big cauldron over the fireplace was boiling. By noon the teams escorting the bride from the bridegroom's had arrived. But it was hard to identify from among the ladies in the teams who the bride was, because she did not dress herself in any specific manner, and all the ladies were gorgeously attired. The men in the teams carried on their backs baskets containing food, wine and gifts. "Every guest has to gulp down a cup of wine at the gate of the host's house" is the initial ritual of a Lisu wedding. A guest coming to attend a marriage ceremony, whether the guest be a male or a female, old or young, on entering the host's house has to drain a cup — a bamboo cup — of the tamped wine and has to say congratulatory and benevolent words to the new couple. From this moment onward, the bamboo cup will be used by the guest alone for the duration of the whole ceremony, and the host will come to every guest repeatedly to fill his (or her) cup with wine.

I had never seen a wedding feast like this

A guest at a marriage ceremony, has to be provided with a bamboo cup for drinking wine at the feast. The girls are seen washing clean many crates of bamboo cups under the direction of an elder.

before. It proceeded in the following manner: The host put in many a big and flat bowl made of plaited bamboo strips plenty of cooked ground corn grains. Spread over the grains were chunks of pork, beef, mutton, and chopped pieces of the entrails of these animals. If the host neglected to put into a bamboo bowl the chopped pieces of a certain internal organ of these animals — say a pig's intestine — the guest who was served with the bowl would good-naturedly tease the host and exclaim in mock surprise, "Why, strange isn't it, the pig our host raised didn't grow intestines?"

A long queue of youngsters was deployed along the passage extending between the kitchen door and the door of the hall upstairs, where the wedding was in progress; they were charged with the duty of passing one by one the bamboo bowls filled with cooked ground corn, grains and meat to those who were in the upstairs hall celebrating the wedding. When such a bowl was passed to the door of the hall, an announcer would sonorously declare, "This is for so-and-so!" Then so-and-so would come forth to receive the share of the food. Of

course, the aged people or those ranking higher in family or clan hierarchy are served the food sooner. The guests did not begin to eat the food the moment it was served. They just poured their shares of food into the baskets they had brought on their backs and hung the baskets on the rows of bamboo pegs fixed to the wall and returned to the seats to resume the singing and drinking. When they felt like eating the food, they just scooped up some grains from within the baskets and devoured them.

Sitting on one side of the fireplace were the elder members of the bridegroom's family, while the counterpart elders of the bride's family sat on the opposite side of the fireplace. When they were ready for proceeding with the nuptial antiphonal singing, the bride's mother started the festivity by singing, "My girl's a little bungler, who often had the rice burned in the cauldron when she cooked. Please forgive her if she bungles again. Please don't be too harsh with her." Then the father of the bridegroom sang in antiphony, "Please don't worry. We're fond of her as we'd our own daughter. If she doesn't know how to cook, she

A guest who comes to the bridegroom's house to congratulate him has to drink a full bamboo cup of wine at the gate before he is admitted. This is an unchangeable ritual of the Lisu wedding ceremony. No guest is exempted from drinking the cup of wine.

may learn it step by step. And we believe she'd become a good and able housewife." In this antiphonal manner, the elder members of both families proceeded to discuss and settle all the specific concerns in connection with the marriage, such as what gifts should be donated to what particular relative. When both sides drifted more and more towards consensus through such an antiphonal negotiation and finally eliminated all the differences between them, they began to hobnob. Those who liked to drink excessively would finish a full cup of wine at a draft; those who were sociable would propose unison toasts to many others. A bridegroom may propose a unison toast to any girl present at his wedding, and likewise a bride may propose a "unison toast" to any boy present at her wedding.

Somebody began to strum his qieben, and some other people began to play their flutes; then all the people in the hall began to perform the Guakeke and Qianeqian dances. The Guakeke dance is characterized by its casual, slow and gentle motions, while the Qianeqian dance is jerky and swinging in its movements,

which are complicated with leaps and bounds. The young people stamped their feet energetically to the rhythm of the music, and the whole bamboo building trembled and creaked under their feet. It was fortunate that the host had already strengthened the building in anticipation. Therefore, the guests danced and sang most heartily.

The day following the wedding was set for the bride to pay a formal call to her parents. The bridegroom sent with her, as a present to his father-in-law, a big pig's head, which was packed in a bamboo-strip crate originally for containing the cooked ground corn grains. The crate was borne to the bride's parents' home by two people who also escorted the bride. Though the bride now was gone for this home visit, the guests turned up at the bridegroom's house to continue their revelry in spite of her absence. The revelry usually went on for three days and nights.

In bygone days, Lisu young people were quite unrestrained in their premarital affairs. In those days their marriages were arranged by their parents; as a result, many young people

The bride and the bridegroom have to drink a union toast from the same cup in the presence of all the guests.

A guest to a Lisu marriage ceremony has to be provided with a proper share of the marriage feast. The picture shows that the host is preparing the wedding feast and dividing it into equal portions for all his guests. A marriage feast usually has to be divided evenly into as many as 100 portions.

The high tide of the marital orgy may continue for days and nights, with all the villagers singing and dancing rapturously around the clock inside and outside the house of the bridegroom.

resorted to fleeing their homes or their weddings in order to shun the nightmare of a coercive marriage and to strive for a union born of true love. Such a desertion from a home or an impending coercive marriage often ended up in bitter memories or unfulfilled wedding hopes. Nowadays, as the living standard and cultural level of the Lisu people continue to rise, arranged marriage as a social phenomenon is dwindling, and the marriage ceremony is increasingly a sign of happiness for the married couple.

The Jubilant New Year's Day   by the Lisu Calendar

I happened to tour the Lisu region during a New Year Festival by the Lisu calendar. According to the "natural" calendar peculiar to the Lisu nationality, one year is divided into 10 months including the blossoming month, bird-chirping month, kindling-the-mountain month, no production month, gathering month, reaping month, hunting month, New Year Festival month, and house-building month. The numbers of days in these months are not equal. By the Lisu calendar, New Year's Day does not fall on any fixed date, but is set annually by their elder people at their own discretion. Their old folks determine the date of their New Year solely on the grounds of their observation of certain phenomena of nature. However, the New Year's Eve by the Lisu calendar must be timed to fall on a night in which the moon must wane to nothingness.

Baba made of polished glutinous rice is an indispensable delicacy of the Lisu people during their New Year Festival. It is made by first pulverizing the polished glutinous rice into flour by tamping the rice with wooden pestles in a mortar, and then by wrapping up pieces of dough made of such flour in patches of banana leaf. The steamed wrappings of the dough are called baba by the local people. To eat baba, you just snap off the thin flaxen string securing the baba wrapping, then remove the wrapping of the patch of banana leaf, and roast the baba over the fireplace. The roasted baba is sweet, fragrant and gummy.

The Lisu New Year Festival lasts generally from seven to nine days. Paying visits, hobnobbing, and dancing are part of the happy routine of these holidays. In this festival period, music, songs and the stampings of dancing feet are audible from early morning till deep night.

There is a popular saying among the Lisu people: "As salt is indispensable to life; so is singing." Truly, their social life withers if they are forbidden to sing. The building of a friendship, the beginning of a romantic attachment, the showing of hospitality to a newlyarrived or leaving guest, the edification of the younger generation, or even the arbitrating of a dispute always relies heavily on singing as a vehicle. On festival occasions and when excited by their wine, the Lisu people sing many more songs than they do at ordinary times. It is no exaggeration that their songs are as inexhaustible as the wine in their breweries. Their singing art includes antiphonal singing, solo performances, and choruses. They sing in praise of their bumper harvest, and they also sing about their bright future. Thrilled by the enrapturing drink in their cups, they may be carried away by their own songs, and at such a moment both the militant and gallant Lisu men and the pleasant and tender-hearted Lisu women will look so exalted and sublime that they are conscious neither of where they are leading the world nor where the world is showing them.

One of the most popular games with the Lisu people during the 10 days of the New Year is shooting at a target made of baba with a crossbow. They suspend a piece of glutinous rice "baba" in the air as a target. He who can use his crossbow to shoot an arrow through the target is supposed to become very lucky and be able to hunt more successfully in the new year. In olden times this game was laden with superstitious belief; now it is practised simply as a sport. All the Lisu males, whatever their ages, are eager to show off their archery in this sport; for them a crossbow is not only a hunting weapon to be kept always at hand, but also an ornament signifying bravery and physical strength. That is why even a little urchin here equips himself with a light crossbow.

Probably the most interesting and stirring event in the New Year holidays is the game played by young men and women on the river bank — a game called "a burial in the sand." There are numerous sand ridges on the banks of the Nu River. In the New Year holidays, young Lisu people from various stockaded villages haunt the banks and play there. Having danced and sung to their hearts' content, the young unmarried women, all in their full dress, simultaneously leave the reveling crowd and betake themselves to a spot some distance away from the crowd for a secret consultation. Then all of a sudden, they dash towards a young man from various directions, swoop down upon him, lift him up and move him away to a pit by a sand ridge. The young man, confident of his own physical strength, struggles with all his might, but he is overwhelmed at last because he is hopelessly outnumbered. He is hurled into the pit, and a young woman immediately covers his face with a broad scarf, while other young women set about throwing fine sand on him until the pit is filled up. His head is left above the sand but his body is completely buried in sand. According to the customary practice in the olden days, at this juncture all the young women have to sit around the pit and cry over the buried young fellow. It is a past belief of the Lisu people that the young woman who cries most heart-brokenly loves him most dearly. But contemporary Lisu people have now formulated among them a new practice. The young women who take pleasure in "burying" a young man in the sand in the New Year holidays are just laughing instead of crying around the "interred" man. Perhaps his authentic sweetheart is the very girl who laughs most lustily at his "entombment."

This game provides the young people with chances for knowing and falling in love with each other, and it also gives expression to their fresh and overflowing vitality. It is permissible not only for the young women to seize and "bury" a young man, but also for the young men to capture a young woman, whether she is married or not, and "bury" her; so even some young mothers are not exempted

from being deposited in a sand pit on such an occasion.

The day I was engrossed in snapping a photograph of the game of mock burial a group of lively Lisu young women unexpectedly closed in upon me, and without further ado they dismantled me of my camera and its accessories and dragged me by hands and feet into a pit. There they laughingly strewed handfuls of sand on me while chattering away merrily over my sprawling body.

The old people sat nearby drinking and watching these frolicking and romping young people, while their memories raced back to the days when they themselves had played the same pranks on each other. Sometimes these old folk would spread out in a circle on the sandy bank and go into their Qianeqian or Guakeke dance. In those holidays the grand canyons of the Nu River were reverberating with the joyous songs and music of the Lisu people all day long.

The Lisu people have other festivals and festivities by the Lisu calendar in addition to

One of the indispensable personal trappings of a Lisu male is his crossbow. The effective range of a strong crossbow can be over 200 metres, far enough to strike a target on the opposite bank of the Nu River.

Even a boy in his teens takes a crossbow with him wherever he goes.

One of the sports in the Lisu New Year Festival is a shooting game for Lisu male adults. They use crossbows to shoot at a piece of *baba* made of cooked polished glutinous rice placed on the top of a tall post. He who can hit the piece of *baba* with the missile from his crossbow is supposed to be very lucky in the new year.

A Lisu girl is inclined to show her affection for a young man by playing an amorous tune on her bamboo mouth organ, made of a piece of very thin bamboo strip or reed. A mouth organ can be used to play very melodious tunes. Every Lisu girl has a bamboo mouth organ in her pocket.

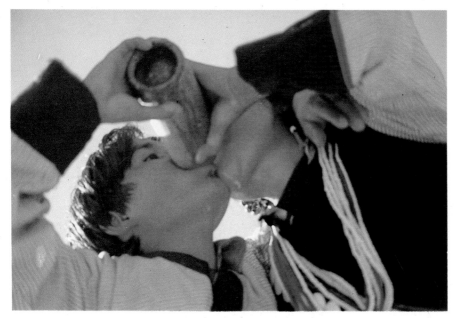

The young sweethearts are drinking from the same cup in a unison toast, a way to pledge fidelity to each other.

Lisu youth playing the game of "a burial in the sand." Girls often drag young men after their hearts to a pit near a sand ridge on the river bank.

In the midst of the girls' ringing laughter the lucky young man is being "buried" in the sand.

Lisu youth dancing merrily on the sandy beach of the Nu River.

the New Year holidays. The Lisu natives of Bijiang and Lushui counties prefer to go to the hot spring and have baths there during the Lisu New Year holidays. They bring their New Year delicacies and luggage with them and pitch tents in the vicinity of the hot spring, and often camp there for a couple of days. During these holidays the singers from the villages within a radius of scores of kilometres of the hot spring converge there to have an antiphonal contest, which is formally termed

the Hot Spring Antiphonal Competition.

The Variegated Lisu Tribe in Tengchong County, Yunnan, observes a festival called "climbing-sword-ladder-festival," which falls on one of the first days of the second lunar month. The festivities on this occasion include fabulous events which call for climbing a sword-ladder and walking on burning charcoal performed by some Lisu male performers; they can walk barefoot and unscathed for some distance on live coals or embers or climb

barefoot up a ladder whose rungs are dozens of swords with their sharp edges turned upwards. Every climber of the sword-ladder has to perform a handstand on the top rung and at the same time fling down five pennons in five directions before he descends. This pennon-flinging ritual is meant as a prayer for the advent of an auspicious new year and for a bumper harvest.

A popular saying with the Lisu people goes like this: "None except the dead should be deprived of the mirth of life." It is quite appropriate to say that the Lisu people should be highly praised for their straightforward, lively, and mirthful nature. They are pioneers, bravely and merrily ploughing, sowing, and reaping in the high fields of the snowy Biluo and Gaoligong mountains and in the deep canyons of the Nu River. They earn their mirthful life by virtue of their own diligence and wisdom.

在滇西北峡谷中

沈　澈　摄影

沈　澈
陆小娅　撰文

*

外文出版社出版
（中国北京百万庄路24号）
民族印刷厂印刷
中国国际图书贸易总公司
（中国国际书店）发行
北京 399 信箱
1989年（16开）第一版
（英）
ISBN 7—119—00567—7/J・399（外）
04500

85—E—279P